No Way to Behave At a Funeral

A Tale of Personal Loss Through Suicide

Noel Braun

Published in Australia by Sid Harta Publishers Pty Ltd,
ABN: 46 119 415 842
23 Stirling Crescent, Glen Waverley, Victoria 3150 Australia
Telephone: + 61 3 9560 9920,
Facsimile: + 61 3 9545 1742
E-mail: author@sidharta.com.au

First published in Australia 2009
This edition published 2009
Copyright © Noel Braun 2009
Cover design, typesetting: Chameleon Print Design

Braun, Noel
No Way to Behave at a Funeral
ISBN: 1-921642-47-5   EAN13: 978-1-921642-47-0
pp274

Her eyes are open
But she cannot see
Beyond the black veil
Drawn across her world
She longs for the bright sun
To shine upon her earth
And banish the bleak dark shadows.
She longs for the gentle breeze
To lift the heavy curtain
That hides the good things in her life
But all she can feel
Are bleak cold winds
That chill her to the soul.

—Noel Braun, 2004

Dedicated to the memory of my cherished wife,
Maris, whose support, encouragement and
quiet confidence inspired me, and continues to do so.

FOREWORD

In Australia, as in many countries, suicide is a leading cause of death. More people die each year from suicide than from breast cancer or in car accidents. Yet it is one of the least talked about health issues in our community.

So when a book like this comes along, I feel compelled to encourage everyone to read it, especially men.

Suicide is devastating, especially for the friends and family of someone who takes their own life. Words can not describe the unimaginable pain that can come when we lose a loved one, or someone close to us. Combine this with feelings of guilt and confusion that can almost engulf us after the suicide of someone we know, and the results can be debilitating.

Books like this can make a difference. The way Noel openly and honestly explores the feelings and deep emotions he felt following the suicide of his wife are powerful and so important for our society. Men in particular often bottle up their emotions, and this can have extremely detrimental effects in the long run. People bereaved by suicide are vulnerable themselves and Noel's story helps us confront this notion and provides us with a pathway to a greater understanding.

The book is also a love story and we journey with Noel, as his relationship with his wife changes, but not in the way you might think. There is a message of hope in this book and the brave way that the author shares his very personal story and his relationship, means we can travel with him. I felt privileged to be a part of his journey.

From the funeral at the beginning right through to learning to live a life with his wife in a new way, the book provides us with an insight into the mind of a man who has experienced life, love and death, and who has arrived on the other side willing to share his experiences.

I felt inspired by his story, and it is a compelling one, around a topic that we desperately need to begin to talk about more openly. I know you will gain a great deal from reading it and I hope it leaves you with one key thought. While suicide is a whole of community health issue and we all have a role to play in suicide prevention, there is always hope, it is the glue that binds us all.

Dawn O'Neil AM
CEO Lifeline Australia

Come on a journey from shock horror and absolute loss, through pain and sorrow, to the cliffs of despair.

Always in the darkness there is a little candle flickering. Love is never extinguished. Slowly, ever so slowly, the light dawns.

You may have made this journey yourself. As you read, may you gain comfort and courage to carry on. Someone you know and love may be on that journey. Now you will have a deeper respect and understanding of them.

Whatever the case may be, you will be changed, encouraged to live each moment of your life with gratitude and grace. These words are not idly written. I know Noel, the man; respect and love him. Noel gives us such a great gift in this book.

Father Peter McGrath cp
Founder Passionist Family Group Movement

PREFACE

A number of reasons lie behind my writing this book. Foremost, I want to honour my wife Maris for the forty-one years that we shared together. I loved her all those years and continue to love her. She is a continuing presence and influence in my life. I like to think of this book as a love story, just a little different from what you would normally find in bookshops, libraries, movies and TV.

Secondly, my hope is that this book may give some comfort and support to those whose lives have been shattered by a loved one's suicide. My heart goes out to them. The suicide of a loved one tops the list of stressors and permanently alters the lives of survivors. What my bereavement has bought to me is vulnerability, but it is a vulnerability that has become a gift for me, and for others, by sharing it. By sharing my pain, my loss, my emptiness, I hope that others who have had a similar experience will share their pain, their grief, their anguish, their feelings of inadequacy and inability to cope.

I hope that the men who read this book will give themselves permission to feel and to weep. Men tackle grief in a different way, often totally avoiding it. Some men build a fortress around their feelings. The pain of loss is just as intense for men as for women, but society praises those men who 'hold up well', who maintain a 'stiff upper lip', who adopt the strong, silent stance we are supposed to display. The belief that pain can be overcome by biting your lip is tied to the fear that it is the only thing that can be done, short of letting down the guard and expressing true feeling, as if the stoic mask provides some protection. On the contrary, instead of shielding against pain, the mask hurts. In hiding pain from others, it has to be carried silently and alone.

Expressing emotion in our own way helps the process of healing. To suppress one's grief and send it underground can be destructive as it can emerge in unexpected ways. In the words of Shakespeare:

Bid sorrow speak; the grief that does not speak
Whispers the o'er-fraught heart and bids it break.
Macbeth, IV, iii

I know I can't tell anyone how to grieve or how to emerge from their grief. Each of us is unique and has to find our own way and in our own time. There is no timetable to tell us how long it will take. However, the lessons I have learned after my wife's suicide may help others to understand their own grief. We had no choice in the tragedy, but we do have a choice in how we respond to it. One important lesson is that there is hope in the worst of situations.

Thirdly, through this book, I would like to thank all those people who helped to ease my anguish. Where would I be without the support of my family and many friends? I am also grateful to the many people I met along the way. Some names I have changed. I have attempted to recreate the many conversations that took place during the period of my story and, although I may not have remembered the exact words, I have endeavoured to record the sentiments expressed. In particular, I would like to thank those friends who have allowed me to reprint their letters. Their letters of support are just a sample of the many I received describing the beautiful person that was Maris.

There is nothing I would not do to have Maris back. I dedicate this book to her memory. She encouraged me to persevere. Her spirit continues to inspire me.

Connect with someone who cares:

Lifeline
13 11 14
24-Hour Confidential
Telephone Counselling
www.lifeline.org.au

Beyond blue
1300 22 46 36
www.beyondblue.org.au

SANE Australia
1800 18 72 63
www.sane.org

CHAPTER 1

I decided I'd try my luck at the Heidelberg Town Hall. The band was good, thumping away vigorously, its steady beat ensuring the floor was always crowded. The night looked bright and promising. The band started up a fox trot. More couples began moving to the floor. There were plenty of girls standing at the edge, waiting for the man of their dreams. Some chatted in groups, giggling together, finding safety in numbers. Others, perhaps more adventurous, were on their own. I looked among them for a suitable partner.

There she was, a tall, slim, dark haired, attractive girl on her own. She stood out from the rest. I couldn't exactly say why. She just stood out. Perhaps she was taller than most. But she was knocking back boy after boy.

'I'll give her a go,' I muttered to myself.

I edged my way around the floor, running the gauntlet of the more adventurous couples flaunting their style with wide ranging flourish.

'Would you care to have this dance?'

She looked at me closely, hesitated for a moment then accepted.

We were awkward at first and danced in silence as we

became used to each other. She did not have much to say. It could have been shyness or maybe she was sizing me up. I made the conversation and asked the questions. She told me her name was Maris. She was 21. She had just commenced her Midwifery Certificate, having completed her general nursing training at Mooroopna Base Hospital in central Victoria. This was her first Saturday night dance in the big smoke. I told her my name was Noel, that I was 26, studying psychology at the University of Melbourne and working as a psychologist and guidance officer with the Victorian Education Department.

'I noticed you were knocking back a few blokes,' I said to her.

'I was waiting for the fellow who had taken me out for a drink at the milk bar to return from moving his car, but by the time you arrived, I decided I'd been stood up.'

We laughed and she seemed to relax. We danced for the remainder of the evening. In fact, you could say I clung to her in case the fellow had returned from shifting his car and wanted to claim her. We got on famously, I thought. After the dance I took her to coffee in South Yarra then home to St Vincent's Hospital nurses' quarters.

'I've taken a shine to that sheila,' I told a mate over a beer. 'I think I could marry her.'

'What do you like about her?'

'She's seems straightforward and genuine. She's fresh and unsophisticated, not like the girls at uni.'

I found out much later that Maris had a different view.

'I'm not going out with that bloke again,' she had said to one of her fellow nurses.

'Why is that?'

'He questions things too much; he's too cynical for me.'

I guess I must have improved and eventually came up to scratch. One night some months later we were parked, cosy in my orange VW beetle, facing St Kilda Beach. The sea was gentle, the waves barely lapping the sand. The moonlight glinted in the water. Our arms were around each other. Was there a better time? I looked across and whispered, 'Maris, will you marry me?'

She whispered back to me, 'I couldn't think of anything nicer.'

CHAPTER 2

In October, 2004 Maris and I were living on Sydney's northern beaches, in the midst of urban bushland. Leafy Frenchs Forest is a beautiful area. Kookaburras woke us with their pre-dawn laughter, galahs and cockatoos made their racket daily. Our two story house overlooked national park and was large enough to raise four children. Built on a steep slope, sixty steps from the front door to the street, its garden wound around the rocks and offered peace and solitude from our busy lives. Maris loved her garden and tended it carefully.

She loved our four children. I loved them, too, but I could see she felt something more. They were her purpose. Like many families, ours was scattered, and it was not often that we saw everyone together, but, for the first time in four years, our children and their partners were all in Sydney.

The family was gathering for Stephen's wedding on November 6th. Stephen, our older son, had been married before. We witnessed the break-up of his marriage, a bad match we thought was doomed from the start. He moved back home, hid from the world in his room and never left his computer. Our son struggled with his anguish, and we were relieved when he finally emerged, began knocking around with his old mates, moved out of home and, after his divorce, courted Anthea, this interesting girl at Macquarie University.

Stephen was a ski enthusiast and told us he planned to propose on top of Mount Kosciusko.

'You might drop the ring in the snow,' Maris had said, ever anxious about Stephen.

Our youngest child, Tim, lived in Melbourne. He had arrived at our place early with his partner Melissa to attend Stephen's bucks' party and to prepare for his job as best man. Although we had spoken on the phone, Maris and I had never met Melissa.

Maris loved family celebrations and should have looked forward to Stephen's marriage with joyful anticipation. She had shared in the planning of Angela's wedding, and had been just as excited about Stephen's first wedding.

Instead, she was dreading this event.

Black clouds of depression cast a terrible veil over her life. She had taken her first anti-depressants twenty years previously. Initially she would suffer for two or three weeks a year, but with time, her bouts of despondency lengthened and became a cruel and dominant master. A relentless pessimism plagued her. I felt impotent as I witnessed the power of depression swamp a normally rational mind with terror and anxiety.

'This wedding's going to be a disaster,' she repeated.

'I'm sure Stephen and Anthea have everything organised,' I replied.

Maris shuddered. 'The reception? A cocktail party?' For her wedding receptions were of the banquet variety where everyone sat down in front of name tags.

'This way the guests can wander about,' I said but she remained unconvinced.

I witnessed her daily struggle. Early morning was the worst. I'd wake, look across and see her eyes wide open, staring at the ceiling, mustering the courage to start the day. I was doing my utmost to accompany her, to support her on her terrible journey.

Maris visited her GP regularly. She was also seeing a psychiatrist and a psychologist, although she was dissatisfied with her psychiatrist and wanted to change. He had increased her medication drastically, but she was getting worse. We talked. She seemed to need me around. We discussed her options.

'A new psychiatrist might change your treatment,' I said.

'He might put me in hospital while I'm being weaned off my old medication and waiting for the new to take effect.'

In mid-October after some careful research and discussion, she chose the names of two psychiatrists. Her first choice was not available until the following year, and the other could not see her until mid November. She was bitterly disappointed.

'I might be dead by then.'

'How do you mean?' I asked.

'I've never been suicidal before, but I am now.'

I'll never forget the knot in my stomach. It would be fair to say I didn't have a clue what to do. 'Think about your appointment with the new psychiatrist. He might put you in hospital.'

She seemed to relax, but I knew that she would require continuing care.

'I'll stay with you all the time,' I offered.

'No, you've got to continue with your normal interests and not feel restricted. What sort of life is that?'

I had enrolled for a training course for the weekend, a Gestalt therapy course with Lifeline.

'I'll cancel the course on the weekend and stay with you instead.'

'No, I want you to go, Noel.'

We tried to lead a normal life. On Tuesday she dined with friends from our church. Maris let on to very few the extent of her suffering, but one of her close friends asked Maris how she was. Maris replied with typical understatement. 'I'm not travelling well.'

Wednesday night we went to the Opera House to see *The Mikado*. She did not want to go but I encouraged her, thinking the outing might make her feel better. She dressed carefully as always. I used to joke that she 'scrubbed up well'.

The weather was perfect, a fine balmy night. We arrived early and admired the view of the harbour and the bridge. We walked arm in arm along the concourse and stopped to listen to the spruikers. We sat in the foyer with a cup of coffee and watched the comings and goings, something Maris always enjoyed. Maris laughed at the antics of the performers and the pretty how-di-do Poo Bah, Nanki Poo and the rest managed to get into. I glanced across at her frequently. She seemed content as we walked back to Circular Quay, admiring the fairy land created by the lighted bridge, surrounding buildings and boats. I was feeling hopeful as we travelled home.

Thursday morning she had a 9 am appointment with her GP. I expected her home early. As the morning advanced towards afternoon, I became agitated and restless. I wandered about the house, frustrated I could not contact her. She had no mobile. Imagine my relief when she appeared out of nowhere in our backyard.

'You had me scared stiff, Maris. Where've you been?'

'I've been looking for a place to jump.'

I can't begin to describe my alarm. It was not a particularly warm day, but I felt the sweat in my arm pits and the smell of fear.

'I checked out the cliffs at Dee Why but I've found the perfect place — the Westfield Car Park at Chatswood.'

I was speechless.

'I'm glad I didn't jump,' she continued in her matter-of-fact tone. 'Besides, I would want to write a note to everyone in the family and by the time I'd done that, I'd have lost the urge.' Then she laughed.

This relieved me immensely. I felt the stomach knots unravelling. I wanted to believe we were over the worst. I slipped into denial, I guess. I wanted to share my concerns with someone. My daughter Jacinta was living with us with her husband Rick but she was preoccupied with her baby, Brody, sick at the time. Maris insisted I do my Lifeline Telephone Counselling shift arranged for the afternoon.

While I was away, she decided to clear out Stephen's room in preparation for my sister Maria and husband Joe who would be arriving the following week for the wedding. Stephen was away with Anthea on pre-wedding visits to country relatives. When I returned home Maris, our daughter Jacinta and I carried his goods to a place upstairs we call the gallery which is used for storage. I checked out Maris. She seemed in good spirits, happy that she had tackled a messy job, the morning thoughts forgotten. She reminisced about the many times she had cleaned up after Stephen, the untidiest by far of our children. I felt optimistic but I was still on edge.

* * *

On Friday morning I woke to find Maris staring at the ceiling.

'Noel, I'm wretched,' she said. 'I don't think I can handle today.' Our grandson Hugh's preschool had organised a Grandparents' Day.

'Hugh would be disappointed if we didn't go.'

'Okay, let's go.' She rolled out of bed and got herself ready with a grim determination.

When we got to the preschool Hugh was delighted to see us. We sauntered around and talked to other grandparents about the great times children have these days. Maris sat with Hugh while he drew and played with blocks, and watched him in the playground digging vigorously in the sand.

'The sandpit is his favourite,' the teacher said to Maris.

Maris always had her camera, a small Olympus. The battery was held in by tape because the battery compartment cover was lost, but it took good photos. She took several snaps of Hugh in action and asked the teacher to take a photo of the three of us.

On the way home we called on our daughter Angela. Maris did not want to go inside and we spoke to Angela on the kerb, but were persuaded because Angela's two year old Eliza was dashing out of the house and threatening to cross the road. Eliza cuddled Maris the whole time in unspoken communication. Maris sat with eyes closed while Eliza rested her head on her lap.

We stopped at the Warringah Council Nursery to look at some native grasses and trees for our garden. Maris enjoyed our garden and whenever I saw her weeding or watering, I knew she was feeling better. When she wasn't, the plants had to fend for themselves. I was no gardener although Maris called on me when there was heavy work to be done. We didn't buy any plants but decided that wallaby grass and a few more eucalyptus would suit our garden.

As we drove home, I sensed from her silence that black clouds were gathering. I glanced across at her. She was staring straight ahead, fatigue was in her eyes.

I chatted about the coming wedding, of all the kids being in Sydney. 'We all love you, Maris.' I reached over to pat her thigh and steered with one hand.

'I know. I'm lucky to have such a loving family and caring husband.' She took my hand.

'I've got a counselling appointment at Lifeline this afternoon. I should cancel it and stay with you.'

'No, Noel, keep your appointment. I'll take things quietly and have a rest.'

* * *

Friday night was a big night. The family assembled at Angela's for a pre-wedding party. Everyone was there except for Stephen and Anthea who guaranteed they would arrive from their country visiting later. Jacinta, Rick and Brody left early in their car as Jacinta was keen to settle young Brody.

Maris and I drove later. Just as we arrived in Angela's street, Maris became very agitated and confused. She seemed terrified, wringing her hands.

'Noel, we have to go back home. Stephen will come home and find all his belongings moved.'

'That's okay.'

'No. He will feel rejected and unwelcome.'

'But Stephen's not going home. He's arranged to come to Angela's first. You can tell him what we've done and why.'

'No. We should go home and put all his things back.'

'What if I ring Stephen's mobile as soon as we were inside?'

'Noel, I need to go to hospital.'

I didn't know what to do. Should I drive straight to Royal North Shore or Northside? I wasn't even sure how one was admitted to hospital. Did you just turn up? 'You've got your appointment with the new psychiatrist in two weeks time. He might put you in hospital,' I said.

'Noel, I need to go to hospital now,' Maris repeated, still wringing her hands.

Both my heart and mind were racing as we sat in the darkened car, Maris in crisis and filled with fear. What could I do? I wanted to do the best for her welfare. At the same time, for Stephen and Anthea's sake, I was frantic for a smooth run, if it was at all possible, up to their wedding.

I took a gamble. 'Perhaps we should go inside. The family's waiting. We can think about hospital later.'

She seemed to accept the idea and reached for her handbag. That gesture of tucking her bag under her arm was so familiar, a signal she was ready for action.

I thanked God Stephen answered his mobile. 'Of course, I'm not concerned. Anthea and I are on our way. See you soon.'

We had a very good night. We met Tim's new partner Melissa, who came up to all our expectations. I could see they were very fond of each other. Stephen and Anthea arrived. The family settled down to the party with lots of music and chatter. We know how to enjoy ourselves, our mob. Maris took out her battered camera. We took many photos and had lots of laughs.

'You kids are worse than the oldies,' I said. 'When you get

together, you reminisce about the old days as if you've all lived a hundred years.'

I was still uneasy and kept a close eye on Maris. But I was relieved to see her smiling. She seemed to be beaming with maternal pride as they told their stories.

During the evening, she took her boys, Stephen and Tim, aside. I watched them in the corner of the lounge room. She held their hands firmly and looked them firmly in the eyes.

'I love you.'

'We love you, too, Mum.'

'I'm so proud of you both. You've chosen such lovely girls as your partners.'

'Thank you, Mum,' they both said.

'I've had a good life rearing my children to be the fine young people you are today.' She gave each of them a pro-longed hug.

Later, I noticed Maris was missing.

'Where's Mum?' I kept saying.

'Are you worried Mum might do something?' asked Angela.

'Yes.' This was the first time I revealed my deep concern.

Angela found her with the grandchildren. Maris adored her four grandchildren. She spent time with them reading and patted Eliza to sleep, which Eliza had never allowed before nor has allowed since. Angela told me she found Maris later sitting quietly in the bedroom, gently rocking herself. 'Your mother's going psychotic,' Maris said.

When it was time to leave there was lots of kisses and hugs from Angela, Guy, Tim and Melissa. I'd had plenty to drink, so Jacinta drove. Maris and I sat in the back holding hands like young lovers. I leaned over and kissed her cheek. She did not respond as she usually did with a reciprocal kiss, but stared remotely ahead, immersed in her inner world.

The street lights flickered across my wife's pale features. Her cheeks looked so soft and fragile. She was my delicate flower that I wanted to hold carefully and protect from all dangers.

— 1 8 —

CHAPTER 3

Saturday 30th was the day of Stephen's bucks' party. It was a warm, humid morning, typical of early summer. While Stephen and friends went paint-balling, I was to attend my training course and late in the afternoon Guy, Angela's husband, and I would join the paint-ballers for dinner.

When I woke Maris was staring at the ceiling. 'I need to go to hospital,' she said.

My racing heart echoed her pain and my head tried to gauge the depth of her terrible anguish. I felt helpless.

She rang in turn her GP, psychiatrist and psychologist, none of whom answered her call. I was distressed about her restlessness. I had to stay with her even though I didn't know how to help her.

I rang Marie, a colleague at Lifeline, who was attending the Gestalt course, and asked her to offer my apologies. Maris seemed to calm herself when I told her I would stay with her.

I showered and dressed and went downstairs to the kitchen. Even when under stress we slip into automatic and go through our routines. Each morning I squeezed us an orange drink. I had hers ready. She went into my home office before coming out to the kitchen.

'I just want to dash up to Terrey Hills to get the books from Ginny,' she said.

This sounded reasonable as I had heard them, both avid readers, discussing the books earlier in the week. 'Have your orange drink and some breakfast first,' I said.

'I want to catch Ginny before she goes out.'

At that moment, I thought she had used the phone to contact Ginny when she went into my office. She took her car keys and dashed out the door to the garage before I could think. This sudden change confused me. I followed her out. I had it in mind to drive her. Too late. I caught a glimpse of her staring ahead as she drove her Blue Nissan Pulsar down our laneway.

She left just on 9 am. Thus began the longest morning of my life.

Tim and Stephen's friends arrived for a barbeque breakfast. The smell of sausages and bacon drifted along our balcony as the young men gathered, chatting and laughing in antici-pation of the day's fun. I tried to reassure myself that Maris would be back soon with the books but as the clock advanced to 10 am dread possessed me. It was as though someone had intruded into a private inner space and violated something precious. Something was terribly amiss.

I mixed with Stephen's friends and tried some small-talk but I couldn't concentrate and wandered around the house waiting for I knew not what (but I really did). I tried to con-ceal my concern from Stephen. I did not want to upset his day. Besides Maris might be back any tick with her books and an excuse. Maybe Ginny kept her talking.

An hour later I looked down from the balcony and saw two police climbing our sixty steps to the front door. The knot in my stomach tightened as I waited for them to reach the house.

'Do you own a blue Nissan Pulsar?' the police sergeant asked.

'Yes, I do. That's my wife's car.'

'There's been an accident. Would you go immediately to Royal North Shore Hospital?'

'What's happened?'

'Got no details. But here's my mobile number.'

I was confused. I couldn't think. Tim and Jacinta, waiting in the background, heard every word.

'I'll drive you, Dad,' said Tim.

'I'll come, too,' said Jacinta.

We drove down the lane in time to see some of Stephen's friends already leaving. As the three of us were driving down Boundary Street, the police sergeant rang.

'Is some one driving you?'

'Yes. Why?'

He didn't answer. There was only one reason why he'd ask such a question. But I tried to fill the vacuum with other possibilities. Another motor accident? Maris had written off her Toyota Corolla back in April. I felt my heart beating furiously at my ribs, as if it was trying to tear itself loose and abandon me.

* * *

'I've been asked to come about my wife,' I said to the clerk at reception, whose jolly mood was completely out of tune with my anxiety. 'Is she alive or dead?'

'Please fill out the admission form,' he said.

With an unsteady hand I completed the details. I couldn't remember my phone number.

We were asked to sit in the waiting room with lots of other people. Through the haze, I sensed a messy confusion as hospital staff, patients and the public came and went. I approached the desk.

'How long do we have to wait?'

'The doctor will talk to you.'

Another endless wait.

Angela arrived, flowing with tears and questions. I hugged her.

'I can tell you nothing. They won't even tell me if Mum's alive or dead.'

Out of the murky bedlam of admission a social worker appeared with the completed form. She beckoned and took us into an adjoining room. As she led us from the bustle to a quiet place, I was shaking. I knew what we would be told, although from her cheerful manner, hope filled my heart. Perhaps Maris was alive but injured.

We found ourselves in a comfortable room with wide sofas and tea making gear in the corner. A place for receiving bad news? Again we waited forever. I wanted Stephen to be present and prayed he was on his way. Through my haze I sensed the room filling with people, social workers and nurses, and a young doctor. She spoke in a quiet, matter-of-fact manner.

'An ambulance was called to the Chatswood Chase Car Park where a woman was found on the pavement, apparently from a fall. The paramedics tried to revive her but brought her to the hospital where she was pronounced dead. I believe she is your wife.'

Ours tears were uncontrollable. The emotion roared out of

us, hit the walls shrieking and rocked around the room. Stephen arrived. The family was complete. Shaking with helpless grief, we hugged each other and wept, unified in our pain. I felt an enormous comfort as we gave each other unconditional support. We were always a close family but in that crowded room, bonds were cemented that will last forever.

'Her body is in the next room,' the doctor said. 'Would you like to see her?'

By now, I was exhausted and had quietened down. 'Yes,' I said.

'I want to remember mum as I knew her,' said Stephen through his tears. Tim and Jacinta agreed. But Angela wanted to see her.

'You might find disturbing the tube the paramedics inserted down your wife's throat in their efforts to revive her. She doesn't look pretty.'

I went in first. What I saw will never vanish in the mists of memory.

My beloved Maris, my cherished sweetheart, on a table, naked except for her wedding ring, but covered by a sheet with arms exposed.

I would like to say she looked peaceful in death, but I could see the grim lines of pain around her mouth, traces of the anguish that drove her to this place. The tube did not disturb me. What did upset me was her left eye half open and, although I guess they had cleaned her up, her beautiful dark hair was messy and the way her eye was turned told me she had suffered a severe blow to the head and incurred extensive internal damage.

I thought I had exhausted my tears but I wept again as grief once more took control. I took her cold hand and spoke.

I can't remember what I said. A jumble of words. I was saying good-bye, I think. While the tears and emotion poured out of me like a torrent and flooded the room, a social worker continued to sit in the corner, hands folded, eyes downcast, noticing everything.

A sharp pain gripped my chest. Doctors would say my body was reacting to shock, but I now know what the poets mean by a broken heart. I could not believe I had lost my Maris, the light of my life. I could not grasp I was no longer one of a couple.

I was alone.

CHAPTER 4

A young police woman, Catherine, appeared and asked some questions. Through my tears and running nose I blurted out the story of the last few days. I was surprised how logical and fluent I was. I seemed in control, as if I had detached myself from reality. I'm sure the calm that possessed me was shock as if someone had injected me with an anaesthetic or given me a pain killer.

Members of the hospital staff were present, although I wasn't sure what their roles were, whether they were performing some function or there out of curiosity to know something of the beautiful woman who had arrived dead on their doorstep. They made supportive comments on what a strong, united family we were. I suppose we were. None of us raved or fired blame at whoever was in the way like some mad gunman shooting at random.

'Could I see Maris again?' I asked.

The social worker led me back into the room. I placed the pansy that Rick had brought from the house in Maris' hand. She loved her pansies. Even in the bad times, she managed, like a glimmer of hope somehow, to care for those little plants.

'I want her to take a tiny part of her garden with her to the Coroner's Court,' I said to the social worker. 'Could I keep her wedding ring?'

A nurse removed it. 'You might like the cross and chain she was wearing.'

The chain was broken but the cross was intact. As I write this, my hand traces the outline of that cross beneath my shirt.

* * *

I made two decisions as Tim drove me home. The first was that I would bury Maris at the Frenchs Forest Bushland Cemetery. Reducing my beloved Maris to ashes in cremation insulted the sacredness of her memory. I couldn't bear the thought of her ashes in an urn gathering dust on an empty shelf. I wanted her to be in a special place, a place I could visit and sit in communion with her in the years to come.

The other decision was to tell the world. I had no sense of shame that Maris had died of suicide. For years, suicide was spoken of in whispers. A stigma is still attached to taking one's life. Some families are reluctant to speak about their loved one, or use euphemisms such as dying 'in tragic circumstances'.

I was outraged. I wanted the world to know that an insidious disease had driven my beautiful Maris to this tragic ending. She had lost confidence, hope and the will to live. I wanted everyone to know of the toll depression inflicts. The demons of despair had ensnared the mind of a peaceful, gentle woman, robbed her of peace and replaced any joy with a daily anguish which nothing, nothing could alleviate.

Inside I was crying but the logical part of my mind kept on working. I guessed I slipped into automatic. There were people to tell. I rang the family — my sister Maria and brother Tom. They made me repeat everything as if the news was too shocking to take in at one go. I left a message on Father Brendan's answering machine. The children were on the phone, too. The terrible news spread rapidly.

For a while I was numb where the anguish had roared before. But then an awful battle began to rage beneath. A new sensation emerged. At first it was in the background like the roar of a distant football crowd or a roll of far-away thunder. It grew in intensity until the noise erupted in a new torment. It was my own voice in accusation, a whisper at first, but eventually screaming.

'Why didn't you listen when Maris needed to go to hospital? Why didn't you stop her when she took her car keys? Why didn't you stay with her if you knew she was suicidal?'

Over and over these accusations raged, causing havoc like an army running amok. I was overwhelmed. Guilt was undoing me. In desperation I tried to set up barriers and suppress the questions but they refused to be vanquished and kept breaking the ramparts and bursting into my thinking. If I wasn't questioning, I was scourging myself.

'I failed you, Maris. If I'd been more vigilant, you'd still be here, instead of in the Coroner's freezer. I've killed you by my own neglect.'

Which was worse, guilt or grief? I'm not sure. Take one serving of regret mixed with a heavy dose of guilt and you get the bleakest cocktail of mental pain guaranteed to blight the strongest.

All that afternoon the noise of battle rolled around as

one accusations vied with the other for the high ground, my rational self forced into dark retreat. I was losing the war. I was succumbing to despair.

Brother Damian, Father Brendan's assistant and the proverbial knight in shining armour, came to my rescue. Damian is a member of the Passionist Congregation. They are an order of monks who administered our parish of St Anthony's. A person of great compassion, he has the benefit of counselling training.

I remember removing my glasses, smearing my wrist over my eyes, squashing the tears, although I felt an occasional stray escape and slide down my cheek. 'I should have taken Maris straight to hospital,' I cried to him.

'Sure, you could have taken her,' he said, 'but, with limited resources so overstretched, they would have taken one look at Maris, who presents so calmly, and either sent her home or just kept her overnight.'

I told Damian of my conversations with Maris.

'It's sounds as if she'd made up her mind to go. If she was intent on suicide, nothing would have stopped her. You could have done nothing.' After a pause he added, 'Perhaps God told her it was time.'

Damian's reassurance banished those horrible demons for a time, as if he had administered another anaesthetic to deaden a pain that I knew was bound to return and counterattack with reinforcements.

'Would you like an announcement made at the weekend Masses?' he asked me.

'Yes, I want our total parish community to know.' I wiped my eyes. 'Maris was loved and respected. Many people would wish to attend her funeral.'

We were fortunate, if that is the right word, that a weekend was intervening between Maris' death and her funeral. The word would spread easily.

I thought of our Stephen. Poor bugger! His bucks' party cancelled, his wedding plans wrecked. What a tragic lead-up to what should have been the most joyful day both for him and Anthea! How we protective parents hope to shield our children from sharp arrows.

I had flashbacks of little Stephen trying to play sport. When God lined up the children of the world to hand out sporting prowess, He stumbled as he passed Stephen. I remember the jeering of the St Ives parents as he swung his skinny five year old legs at the soccer ball and tripped, the impatience of the head teacher at his primary school, the irritation of the tennis coach at Stephen's claims that his tennis racket had a hole in it. Fortunately, God handed Stephen a few brains which he made good use of at secondary school and university.

I could see how happy he was with Anthea. I wanted them to have a great day, to shield them from Maris' suffering but my efforts were a devastating failure. If there was any good news that day, it was Stephen and Anthea's decision.

'Dad, we're going to go on with the wedding,' Stephen announced later in the afternoon.

I was so relieved. 'That's great. I was worried you might want to postpone it.'

Angela, Jacinta and Tim agreed.

'Life has to go on.' I added. 'I know it's an old cliché, probably quoted after every death, but it's full of wisdom.'

A huge wave of emotional turbulence had struck the family. We were devastated, striving to make sense of the day. My four children were with me. If ever we needed to cling to each other, this was the time. We sat around the kitchen table where Maris had served so many meals. Tim ordered pizzas. Jacinta found some beers. We needed them.

'Mum was so intense last night, the way she spoke to us,' said Tim.

'I think she was saying good-bye,' added Stephen.

As the beer started to lift our sombre spirits, we told a few stories.

'Mum loved the Sydney Swans,' Jacinta reminisced.

'She sure did. We went to all the home games.'

'Mum was always telling us of your behaviour, Dad. It was embarrassing.'

I found myself laughing, actually laughing. I couldn't disagree with that. I am a passionate supporter, shouting for joy and waving my arms when the Swans score a goal, and loudly abusing the umpires for their countless mistakes.

'Membership for next year's due this week. I'm going to renew Mum's ticket,' I said in between slices of pizza.

'I'll come with you, Dad,' Angela and Jacinta chorused.

The kids wanted to discuss Maris' sisters, Catherine and Loretta. As young children, they were only vaguely aware of the problems they created. Both had died of suicide, Catherine fourteen years previously, Loretta the year before. Catherine was diagnosed as bi-polar, Loretta suffered from depression and compounded her illness through drug and alcohol addiction. Their problems were evident in the dramas they created.

'Those two were crazy,' Angela said, drawing on childhood memories. 'Mum was always the sane one.'

'Yeah, Mum kept her suffering to herself. She'd drop everything to respond to their cries for help,' I said, filling in some of the detail. 'I don't know how many times Loretta was admitted to hospital. It got so routine I was almost blasé when I took the call on the latest calamity. I'd get into trouble with Mum for forgetting to pass on the message.'

Father Peter McGrath arrived and shared our pizza. He, too, is a member of the Passionist Congregation, known to Maris and me since our arrival in Sydney twenty-five years previously. Once the Pastor at our church, he lived apart from Brendan and Damian. His amazing gifts of compassion enabled him to bring solace to the most distressed of people.

'Gosh, Father Peter was in a mess,' commented Jacinta, after he had left.

'Yes, he was more than just a priest to Mum. He was a friend. He's had problems with depression himself. He understood Mum's internal struggles. He knew what she was going through.'

As we retired to bed, I realised that this night would be the first on my own. Maris would never share the bed with me again, a thought I could not grasp. I stood in the doorway staring at the bed. Despite her anguish that morning she had made it neatly as she did every other morning. It looked so ordinary, this essential tool of our life together.

Maris' clothes from the day before were still draped on a chair. A basket of ironing stood in the corner. The walk-in wardrobe was full of her clothes. She dressed well, my Maris. The cupboard was full of her cosmetics and toiletries. She took care in 'doing her face'.

For her birthday that year I bought her some talcum powder. The sales lady talked me into buying some shower mousse saying it was like velvet to the skin. The price was outrageous. Maris hadn't used it. I handled the container and thought about that birthday and many others. I wanted to keep everything as it was, as if Maris had only gone on a holiday.

The demons returned in full force. Like an invading army, desolation and guilt took possession. As I lay in bed conscious of the space next to me I was powerless to stop the recriminations and blame. Why didn't I stop Maris from driving off for that supposed appointment at Terrey Hills? All night long the battle raged. I slept fitfully and each time I woke the realisation flashed through my mind like a streak of lightning. I reached out and felt nothing. At one time, in my half-awake state, I reached over and felt something but it was only her pillow which had somehow travelled down the bed.

We would normally cuddle one into the other and find comfort in each other's body warmth. She would chide me for my cold feet and complain if I placed them on her before they had warmed up. I would run my hand over her bottom and whisper to her how lovely it was. I would feel her breasts and tell her what nice tits she had. I remembered the soft down on her neck. Our gentle conversations, dancing in whispers, came back to me.

I would begin a request with, 'Sweetheart?' and she would reply, 'Yes, my love.' I indulged myself in sweet memories of the many times we made love.

One occasion stands out. In the days when I was a yuppie and drove a BMW we stayed a night in Merimbula. I woke early and went for a run on the beach like good yuppies do while Maris stayed in bed. I returned and had a shower. I stood by the bed naked feeling fresh and frisky and Maris suggested that instead of getting dressed I should join her.

* * *

I woke to emptiness as if I were on a vast barren landscape. I stared at the ceiling as Maris did, the light filtering in from the dawn. Black thoughts hammered me, all starting with 'if only'.

I tried to visualise what life after forty-two years of marriage would be like on my own. I couldn't. We had been in equilibrium, in mutual support, not realising how much we supplemented each other. We had been like two walls in a house supporting each other. One had been pulled out. Now the whole structure was caving in.

The early morning dose of grief, guilt and despair was too much. I resorted to self-deception. Maris was away and would be back. She was already up, having a shower. She was downstairs having her breakfast or sitting in a chair at the window watching the day.

I made the bed inexpertly. I did not have Maris' skills. She had her nursing training and followed the hospital routines of many tucks and turns. I had to recall my army experience, my National Service days where we would receive penalties if we young conscripts did not make our beds properly. It took me several mornings to get it right, to approach the same neat shape that Maris always managed to achieve.

Each morning I took four oranges and squeezed a drink for the two of us. In the kitchen I automatically reached in the refrigerator for the oranges and realised with pain that I only needed two.

Squeezing those two oranges had huge significance. From now on I would be making a drink for one and only for one. We had a ritual of sharing breakfast, making tea and toast for each other, sharing a banana on our cereal. I would collect the *Sydney Morning Herald* and the *Manly Daily*, split them and we would read them over our breakfast.

Never again, Maris! Never again!

I would be making tea and toast for one. No longer the ritual of cutting a banana in two, and slicing the flesh over two bowls of cereal. I would have a whole banana. I would have the papers to myself. I would have my breakfast alone.

The reality of a sunless life was sinking in. I was facing the first day of a new world. A third decision! There was no way of dealing with my grief that would make it painless. It just had to be endured. What could I do to stop it from destroying me? I had seen bereaved people build a wall around themselves. Others had taken to medication or to alcohol to dull the pain and worsen the problem. Facing my emotions full-on was the best means of coping. I should be ready to confront all situations, unpleasant or otherwise.

'Will you come to church with me. I need you,' I said to the family. 'It'll be an ordeal.' Father Brendan would announce the news. People would offer condolences but also ask questions. Some would be gentle and tuned in; others would be clumsy. They'd want to know all the detail and trample through like elephants. But my family agreed.

* * *

As we walked from the car park for the 10 am Mass, people from the 8.30 am Mass were still gathered over their post-Mass tea and coffee. They knew. At another time I would have approached the church self-consciously, aware that all eyes were on me, but that morning I couldn't have cared less if I was the centre of attention of everybody or nobody.

I didn't seek this notoriety. I would have given everything to be walking with Maris, just another couple, as we had done every Sunday for years. Some of these people scurried away to their cars as if to avoid me. I did not mind. I didn't care much if they spoke to me or not. They would have been coming to terms with the shock and not expect to see me. They would have been uncomfortable, unsure what to say. Many people avoid speaking of death, regardless of the cause, but when it comes to suicide they are reluctant to say anything.

Some approached me. They did not say much but showed their support and were open to my emotions. They looked into my eyes and knew how I felt. Father Brendan made the announcement. I felt the tears roll down my cheeks. I don't recall much more of the Mass. A young boy made his First Communion, but I was in too much haze. As I went to Communion I was acutely aware that Maris was not with me. The kids went with me. I thank God for my family.

Outside after Mass, people were incredulous. They could not believe Maris suffered from depression and was so deeply troubled. 'Perhaps she was pushed,' said one lady. 'I just can't imagine Maris taking her own life. It must have been an accident.'

We had visitors that afternoon. They came with casseroles and cakes, and soon the freezer was full — good practical help for a family in crisis. Over many cups of tea I retold the story of the last few days. I needed to tell it. To many of the people Maris had delivered a casserole herself. Visitors told us how she had supported them. I heard many stories that afternoon of Maris' kindness. People asked if Maris had left a note. We hadn't found any.

The phone rang again. 'You can collect the Nissan Pulsar,' said the policeman on the other end of the line.

'Where is it?' I asked.

'It was on the top floor of the car park. It's at the station now. We've put your wife's handbag back in the car.'

'I'll go and get Mum's car,' volunteered Tim.

When he returned he handed me Maris' bag. It contained about $100 in cash, all her credit cards, and her driving licence. Two Chatswood Chase car park receipts told their story after she drove down the lane at 9.00 am. One was stamped 09.19, the other 09.57. Instead of going to Terrey Hills, she had driven to Chatswood, entered the car park, come out and returned. What was she thinking when she left the car park? Where did she go? What was going through her mind when she returned? The ambulance was called at 10.10 am so she wasted no time once she found the car park roof. What was she thinking in her last moments?

In bed that night, like all nights, I automatically picked up my book. It happened to be Elizabeth Jolley's *The Well*. Underneath was a card, the Fathers' Day card which Maris had given me in September. How did it get there beside my bed? Was it there all the time and I hadn't noticed? Or did Maris put it there as a farewell message? I threw *The Well* aside and read the card over and over. A flood of emotions brought on the tears, the sadness, the love, the regrets, the guilt.

CHAPTER 5

My husband, My Love, My Best Friend
You're a wonderful husband, and I love you
For so many reasons
That it's hard to know
Where to begin
You're loving, supportive and sensitive
And I find comfort in knowing that
No matter what happens
You'll always set aside time for me.
You're a wonderful father,
Patient and understanding,
And I can tell by watching you
How much you enjoy being a parent.
You're my partner, my lover and my best friend…,
And everyday that we share
I discover more and reasons to love you.
Happy Father's Day

lack thoughts of regret darted through me again that night. They swooped out of nowhere and flashed away just as quickly, chattering with a voice that accused me of neglect, stupidity, ignorance and indifference to Maris' suffering. Somehow I survived the tormenting hours.

The kookaburras began their day with their derisive laugh. I glanced across the bed, then closed my eyes, trying to put off for a few seconds the vacuum of Maris' absence, willing her back. I opened my eyes. Still an empty bed.

I got up to face the day.

A lot had to be done. Remnants of that calmness that comes with shock once more took over. Certain people had to be contacted. The first was an undertaker. I rang Chris Lee, recommended by Father Peter, and we arranged to meet later that morning.

I rang Fiona, Maris' psychologist.

'Maris won't be keeping her appointment tomorrow.'

When I told her why, I could hear the distress in Fiona voice.

'Maris tried to ring you Saturday.'

'I was with one of my boys at his sport. But I had my mobile with me. I would have certainly seen Maris that day.'

Maris had only rung the home number. That missed opportunity sent a sharp blow to my chest. 'Maris kept saying she wanted to go to hospital but I wasn't sure of the procedure for admission,' I said.

Fiona sighed. 'It's just a matter of turning up.'

Her reply sent me spiralling. I felt as though my ship had struck a rock and I was thrown into the water, drowning in a sea of regret, heavy splintered beams striking me on the head and crushing me. If only I had taken Maris straight away to the hospital. If only...

I felt the vice-like grip on my heart — that broken heart sensation. I could hardly breathe. I will torture myself with this regret for ever, I thought. And I deserve such torture because I failed Maris through unforgivable ignorance.

I guess Fiona knew I needed help. 'Come and see me tomorrow,' she said calmly. 'You take the appointment instead.'

I accepted. I needed to talk and I figured Fiona wanted to talk as well.

Next I forced myself to ring the psychiatrist. I was never happy with him. I found his privacy policy irritating. Even his receptionist didn't want to know me. I had accompanied Maris to some of her appointments and sat in the waiting room. The psychiatrist never wanted to speak to me.

Maris had looked around for a psychiatrist in June. Although she was happy with her GP, who prescribed her Endep, she felt that if the dose was to be increased, she had reached the limit that a GP could safely prescribe. The psychiatrist increased the dose in stages until it was five times higher. But it gave her no relief. In fact, she got worse.

Since her death I have read articles that suggest some of the newer antidepressant drugs do more harm than good. Maris chose her older psychiatrist because she reasoned he might be happy to stay with Endep, which is described as an old fashioned drug.

I could feel my anger rising, a new emotion to date. I was angry about the privacy policy and that my view, as the person closest to Maris, had never been sought. The receptionist answered. I announced myself as Maris' husband and began by saying, 'I assume that doctor would not speak to me.'

'That would be correct.'

I was angry and responded brutally. 'Okay, just tell the good doctor my wife took her own life on Saturday, and if he wants to ring back, he can.'

I slammed down the receiver. I hurt my hand but I barely noticed.

The psychiatrist rang back within minutes. I had calmed down and was courteous. He sounded surprised. I asked if others of his patients had taken their lives.

'It doesn't happen often,' he replied with what I thought was a sense of relief. I could almost hear him thinking, 'This woman has spoilt my record.' He said he was referring to his notes which indicated he treated Maris for depression, the increase in dosage, etc. She had not told him she had suicidal thoughts. I did not detect any sense of caring in this man. I felt he was more concerned with himself and his own record. I became brutal again and said, 'With great respect, my wife was not happy with you. She had already made an appointment with another psychiatrist for next week.'

'I never gained her trust,' he replied.

That was the extent of the conversation. No hint of regret, no expression of condolence or support. Perhaps I misjudged this man. But at the time I imagined him closing Maris' file and dusting his hands. Meanwhile we, the family, were left to deal with our despair.

When I rang Caroline the GP I received concern and compassion. She had known the family for many years. Whenever Maris was down, she made an appointment with Caroline and discussed the dosage of her medication.

Then I rang the Lifeline office. I had an overnight shift on Tuesday. On an overnight, you expect to hear from people with depression and perhaps from someone who is suicidal.

'I don't think I should do this shift,' I said to Donna, the supervisor.

'Absolutely not. Take time out.' Lifeline has a policy of care for its volunteers. Counsellors must look after themselves. You need to have some emotional resilience for telephone counselling but even the most robust can be fragile and vulnerable at times.

I was vulnerable. Nothing in my experience, none of my training, had prepared me for these overwhelming emotions of grief that surged like waves through my body. I needed the support of those I trusted and loved. I felt like a helpless child, needing to be held, comforted and sheltered.

It was a relief. Instead of being 'strong' and independent, I was admitting my limits, seeking help and allowing others to carry my burdens. There was no need to be a brave little boy. I didn't want a stiff-upper lip. I used to be an ordinary bloke doing ordinary things like putting out the bins and paying the phone bill. But now I was struggling to come to grips with an extraordinary, incomprehensibly tragic event. I was flailing around, disoriented, much like the proverbial fish on the hook gasping for air.

* * *

Despite incessant rushes of emotion like pounding waves threatening to drown me, I found a surprising strength in those first days when I needed to muddle through what had to be done. Sometimes we humans can manage catastrophes better than minor irritations.

The undertaker arrived. Chris Lee was very courteous, had a quiet air of confidence and was a person you felt you could trust. His years of dealing with people at a very emotional time was evident in his manner and the way he went about showing us photos of coffins and accessories. He did not push us to buy the most expensive. I can imagine the temptation to up sell to a vulnerable family who want the best for their deceased loved one. We discussed the options — burial or cremation. Burial was twice the price. But I wanted a place where I could visit her. The cemetery was only 3 kilometres from home, within walking distance.

It was fortunate we had consulted a financial planner some years previously. Maris always trusted Brett because he was a country boy. Maris was a country girl herself, from the Shepparton area in Victoria. Her theory was that country folk are more genuine and honest. I liked and trusted Brett, too. He had recommended maintaining a cash fund for unexpected demands. So I had money immediately available. Using it for Maris' funeral was as remote from my thinking as it was possible to get. We also had some money for Stephen's wedding and for a trip. Maris and I enjoyed travelling and we had planned a trip to France and Spain and, had Maris not slid so deeply into depression during 2004, we would have already taken the holiday.

So through good financial planning I had the money immediately available to cover both Maris' funeral and Stephen's wedding. It was a tiny relief to know that even though my world had collapsed, I did not have to worry about finance.

Chris Lee put Angela, Jacinta and me in his car and we took a drive to the cemetery. We inspected the lawn and the monument section.

'Mum among the monuments would have some pretty

tatty neighbours,' I concluded after looking over the ornate graves with their urns and angels. 'The lawn's much nicer.'

The girls agreed. So we opted for the lawns, beautiful with bushland sneaking through the neat level grass. The sunny day was full of bird life. The magpies warbled. Some noisy Major Mitchells arrived, their racket making a joke of our human tragedy. We chose a plot near a seat donated by a family in memory of their son.

'Perfect!' I said to the girls. 'In the future I can walk to the cemetery to visit Mum, and rest on the seat while talking to her.'

We hugged each other and shed a tear, standing on Maris' future resting place.

Back at the house, the flowers began to arrive, and not in small bunches. There were substantial wreathes as well as displays of magnificent exotic flowers arranged on wooden bases. When the dining table was covered we had to find space on the floor.

'I should say to people not to spend so much money on flowers,' I said to Angela. 'They could donate the money to Lifeline instead.'

'No, Dad. Don't deny Mum's friends. They want to show how much they loved her.'

The cards and letters arrived, too. Our letter box, used to receiving one or two letters a day, was too small to handle the volume, and after each delivery we had a box stuffed with mail. We had to recover letters that had fallen into the bushes. Each day the volume grew.

The mail increased so much that Rick offered to build us a larger letterbox. While I was grateful for his generous action, and knew he was trying to be useful in the midst of a family in crisis, it sent me down a spiral. I did not want a new letter box, however beautifully made. I was happy with my old cedar wood box. It used to be quite adequate, but now it was ill-equipped, like me, to handle the emotional turbulence that swept through my psyche, my whole being, or to face the enormous void that had opened in my life.

More visitors turned up with casseroles. I was stunned at people's generosity. Maris had made many casseroles herself over the years, so it was now our turn to benefit. I repeated the story of Maris' depression many times. I did not mind. Talking helped me. I didn't fit the male stereotype of being the strong silent type.

I wanted Father Peter to be involved in the funeral because he was our former pastor and a close friend, but it wasn't so simple. There was tension between him and Father Brendan. Brendan reminded me of a young MBA graduate in his first management job, keen to demonstrate he was in charge. Father Peter was a maverick and somewhat unpredictable so I could appreciate Brendan's discomfort whenever Peter was around. I wanted the two priests to concelebrate Maris' requiem Mass. That would require a little negotiation. I rang Brendan.

'Brendan, I'd like a concelebrated Mass with the two of you, if possible, as our present and previous pastors.'

That's no problem,' said Brendan. I was preparing myself to ask the next question, but Brendan beat me to it.

'Would you like Peter to be the main celebrant?'

Exactly what I'd hoped for! I felt jubilant as I hung up the phone, out of proportion to the event, a tiny piece of good news in a week of disaster.

* * *

Stephen and Anthea came and went, arranging the final details of their wedding. I was worried that they might be missing an opportunity to grieve.

I may sound logical and rational describing these arrangements, but all the while my emotional side was playing havoc, doing a great job of undermining the fragile surface structure. A battle between light and darkness was raging underneath. Intense apprehensions rushed towards me, not as an orderly crowd, but as disorganised, random, pugnacious and destructive hordes. I was frequently in tears, those pervasive guilt feelings were never far away, and the thought that we shouldn't be doing this was always in mind. At one point, sitting alone at the kitchen table, I exploded.

'Mum should be here with us now, looking forward to your wedding,' I said to Anthea, who happened to come into the room. 'She should be showing off the beautiful silver scarf she's bought to wear. The ladies of the family should be discussing what they would be wearing and showing off their finery, offering to loan this or that accessory.'

Anthea put her arm around me. I was learning to accept support from others.

That morning Chris asked for a photo to place on Maris' coffin and for a bookmark he provided as part of his service. I thought of a photo which Angela had taken. About a month before Maris died, Angela visited. She had her camera.

'Let me take a photo,' she had said.

We cuddled, heads close together.

'Now, act like you're sixteen year olds.'

We turned to each other and kissed. For a brief moment, Maris' load seemed to lift. She enjoyed the fooling around and joined in the laughter. Angela gave us copies. I liked the first photo because of the smile Maris had managed despite her intense pain. I had my arm around, cuddled in close. Our hair was mixed.

I showed this photo to Chris.

'I can cut you out and reshape Maris' head so that you would never know you were there,' said Chris.

Simple, well-intended words, but what an impact. The photo was cut in two. We were separated. Once we were one. Our lives were shared. Now my image had been amputated and Maris was on her own, just as I was.

Yes, I was amputated. I had lost half of me. I felt dismayed, as if part of me had been cut away. Maris was always at my side — at dinner, in the car, at church, in bed. We were one, but now we had been hacked apart. It was as if the arm I placed around her had been severed.

I had Maris' appointment with Fiona that afternoon. I had a special relationship with her. About 10 years previously, she contacted me as a psychologist she found in the regional phone book. She had emigrated from South Africa and was keen to find out more of the local scene. She had contacted a number of people but I was the only one to respond. I gave her some local knowledge and over the years referred a number of inquiries to her as my practice at the time was industrially rather than clinically based. Back in June Maris had suggested she should see a psychologist, and I thought of Fiona. Maris saw her weekly and more often if she felt the need. Although patient and professional, they became friends.

Fiona burst into tears as soon as I entered. Our meeting was for the benefit of us both. I did not expect her to tell me much because of the professional relationships and privacy requirements. However, she mentioned that Maris had spoken highly of me and the support I gave her. This reassured me for I continued to think I was a bastard for letting her down.

'I failed Maris by not responding,' I said through tears. 'I know from my knowledge of grief counselling that it is normal for the bereaved to have guilt feelings, but I'm really, really guilty.'

Fiona made three points, similar to Brother Damian. 'If you had taken her to hospital, they would have noted her calm manner, perhaps kept her overnight and discharged her.' She handed me a box of tissues and kept talking. 'Second, Maris had probably already decided to take her life. On her last visit, Maris bought me a bunch of flowers and made a special point of saying thank you. Thirdly, think of all you did for Maris, not what you didn't do.'

Fiona's comments did wonders. I needed to be told over and over that I had done everything that was possible. The deep wounds of regret would probably continue to ache and never heal completely but at least the sharp bitter edge of my guilt was being blunted. Even now my guilt is like a mob of wild demons watching me from the darkness, unmanageable, ready to goad me at any time with malevolent intent.

CHAPTER 6

Dear Noel,

I can't begin to understand how you and your family are feeling or what you are going through at this time, so I will only talk about my own feelings. I spoke with Maris last Wednesday at Mass. She explained that she hadn't been at meditation because she had been caught up with things at home. She went on to talk about the photos I had taken at the fete and other ordinary things. She seemed so calm and normal that the news on Saturday was just totally unbelievable.

The shock and grief suffered by so many of us is a testament to the beautiful person that Maris was. I will remember her for so much — her calm presence at our Wednesday morning meditations; her lovely, warm and empathetic sharing at Time Out where she talked a bit about her struggle with depression — but didn't give away very much; the warm comfort of her hugs at the Kiss of Peace.

Your Maris was a beautiful and loving presence in my life whose calm face belied her pain. For her to end it the way she did, she must have been suffering terribly. My faith tells me that she is safe in the warm embrace

*of our loving God and that she is totally at peace. I take
much comfort from that and my memories of Maris will
be precious ones of the very special person she was.*

*Noel you are a wonderful man and I hope and pray
that you may find much comfort in our God and in the
loving prayers and support from the many people who
love you.*

Love and prayers always,
Miriam

S t Anthony's has a beautiful setting. The building
itself is simple. It is set on a large, open block
with white trunked eucalyptus giving it a feeling of space and peace. Inside and outside merge through
large glass walls and the sounds of nature, the bird calls and
the wind in the trees, are never far away.

I was thankful that the Catholic Church showed more
understanding these days and had changed its attitude
towards suicides. Not long ago the church forbad the burial
of suicides on 'sacred ground'. How countless families must
have suffered from this astounding lack of compassion. No
wonder people were ashamed to admit their loved ones had
died in this way. I sometimes wonder why I still belong to the
Catholic Church for the atrocities it has committed down
the centuries in the name of religion. In contrast, the church
Maris and I knew at St Anthony's welcomed everyone — sinners, divorcees, gays, suicides, the lot. The Passionists placed
people before rules. My pastors, Peter, Damian and Brendan,
had shown great understanding and compassion. Equally, I
knew many people had gone out of their way to make Maris'
funeral a fitting farewell.

The church was full. Every seat was taken and people had to stand outside and look through the windows. I saw many familiar faces. There were many I didn't recognise.

Angela, Jacinta and some of their friends stood at the entrance and gave everyone a booklet and an orchid. I worried there wouldn't be enough.

My pain was sharp when I saw Maris' coffin. Up to this moment, everything seemed so unreal, but we now were facing the harsh cold reality. An enlarged version of the amputated photo sat on the lid, together with her Sydney Swans cap and scarf.

Father Brendan, as the Parish Priest, welcomed everyone and then handed over to Peter. The large crowd, Peter said, was an indication of the love and esteem with which Maris was held. He admitted he had been deeply affected by Maris' death. They were kindred spirits in their fight against depression. He invited me to deliver the eulogy.

I was not nervous as I stood at the dais. I read in my friends' and family's faces support, warmth, love and compassion. It did not matter if I broke down and wept in front of everyone and messed up my delivery. They were all on my side.

I knew exactly what I wanted to say.

I thanked everyone for coming; their presence was an acknowledgment of the way Maris touched so many people. I explained the reason for her photo on the back cover of the booklet. She was a self-effacing person who preferred the background to the limelight. She used to say she would rather go to Siberia than speak in public. I mentioned the orchids. They were a symbol of Maris. I invited people to take them home. It was very fitting that Maris was being buried from St Anthony's in the Fields. This was her beloved church.

She loved the Passionists, the people, the family groups. She had been involved in developing and promoting the Family Group Movement. She had been a member of various committees over the years. When our family came to Sydney 25 years previously, Maris gave the place three years. St Anthony's kept us here.

I could read the question in people's eyes: why did Maris take her own life? I offered them an explanation.

Depression is a vicious affliction. Maris used to say, 'Give me a bout of cancer any day.' Early morning was the worst time. I read the poem. Few people knew of her anguish, but I knew and felt helpless as I watched her daily struggle. She never gave into herself but reached out, helping people in her quiet unobtrusive way.

She tried everything — hypnotherapy, acupuncture, medication, tapes, meditations, exercise, gardening, innumerable self-help books, attending courses, even sardines for the omega3. I had to eat the sardines, too. I'll never eat another one.

She worsened over her last two weeks. I tried to walk with her, but her pain was unbearable. I saw all the signs of her terrible anguish.

I told the gathering I was a Lifeline counsellor. That I had talked to many suicidal people, attended training courses in suicide intervention. Part of my motivation for joining Lifeline in the first instance was to give me an orientation that might help Maris one day because of her family background. I spoke of her two sisters, Catherine and Loretta. It was a sad irony that despite all my awareness, I failed to save my own wife. Even though I had been trained to help people with suicidal thoughts, I couldn't prevent tragedy in my own home.

If ever there was good timing for her death, it was now. Earlier in the year, only Angela was in Sydney. Jacinta was in Idaho, Stephen was at Perisher, Tim in Melbourne.

But the family was all in Sydney for Stephen's wedding to Anthea. I mentioned that Maris lying in her coffin was dressed in her 'mother of the groom' outfit, including the silver scarf, and that Anthea would wear Maris' engagement ring on her day. We had had a lovely gathering the previous Friday evening, the first time all the family had been together in four years. Maris spent time with each of the children. In retrospect, we felt she was saying goodbye.

It was time to conclude. All of my words are so inadequate, I said. After forty-two years I could not imagine life without Maris. But it was not the end. Maris was still here in the way she had touched all of us and in our memories. She left us an example of bravery in handling this incredible affliction, as noble as another person's fight with a terminal illness. The memory will live on. We will remember her for the lovely person she was. Besides, we are people of faith. How despairing and empty it would be without that faith. We hope. We believe. We use beautiful poetic images like going home safely, resting at peace, being in the arms of a loving and forgiving God. I believe Maris still exists, we don't know how. We believe she is still with us. We use words such as soul and spirit to describe her presence.

I was thankful for my eloquence, my ability to articulate and express my feelings, to be open to and about my emotions. In earlier years I would have bottled up and been more stoic. Maris had taught me so many things about expressing my emotions. She told me it was alright for men to cry.

The eldest of our children, Angela was the next to speak.

'Mum always said that Jacinta, Stephen, Tim and I were her greatest achievement. Her life's work. I am sure you will agree she did an excellent job. She gave us space and freedom to spread our wings whilst always remaining close by ready to comfort, support, laugh, cry, cook, clean, baby-sit, chat, nurse. The list never ends. What lucky children Tessa, Hugh, Eliza and Brody are to have such a devoted Gran. When I asked my six year old daughter Tessa last night what she loved about Gran she said her hugs and kisses.

'I don't need to tell you what an amazing friend she is. You already know. I don't need to tell you what an amazing woman she is. You already know. But I will tell you how privileged we are to have received the unconditional love of our beautiful mother.'

I asked Janne to deliver a final reflection. Maris always regarded Janne as her best friend. They had shared so many confidences over the years. Janne was not well and struggled with a debilitating illness. I remember when we came back from Melbourne after attending the funeral of Maris' sister Loretta, Janne had said to Maris, 'Don't ever do that to me.' Maris assured her that she never would, just as she had assured me.

Janne hated public speaking as much as Maris, but she agreed despite her concern that she was likely to break down in public. But she managed and delivered her message beautifully.

'Many years ago Maris and I did a course together studying Scott Peck's book *The Road Less Travelled*. It was the beginning of a journey for us both, endlessly searching for ways of dealing with difficult moments in our lives. My healing started when I was diagnosed with Addison's Disease but for

Maris the problem wasn't as easily addressed. Maris went looking everywhere for something or someone to help ease this wicked illness called depression which kept overwhelming her and dragging her down. On the way to work recently I heard Petria King from Quest for Life talk about living in the moment and I rang Maris to tell her about it. And in her matter of fact way she said, "I've tried that." We laughed about it together, she had tried everything.

'So many of us here today will have experienced the Angel in our midst who phoned everyone in the family group to chat and catch up on their news, who listened to all our woes, who dropped around with a chicken casserole if she thought we needed one, who gave of herself always without expecting anything in return, who never took sides, who welcomed us all with her wonderful smile, who accepted us all equally and unconditionally, who was suffering from this terrible, terrible illness.

'We *all* tried so hard to keep her with us but it was not to be.

'Maris, you are *still* an angel in our midst — and I love you.'

Father Peter called the four kids and me to the altar and presented us each with a candle, a large one for me and smaller versions for the children — symbols of Maris. Another occasion for tears. I already knew where I would place my candle.

The service concluded with *I can see clearly now,* lyrics and music by Johnny Nash. As I followed Maris' coffin outside, my feelings of sadness, loss and abandonment intense, I realised just how many people were present. The farewell service was to take place at Frenchs Forest Bushland Cemetery.

Most people I expected would not follow us but remain at the church for afternoon tea. However quite a few piled into their cars as we did. Guy drove me and the four children. As we left the church grounds I was amazed to see a guard of honour at the entrance. It was the Catenians. I realised they were there for me, one of their fellow brothers.

I felt the sensation in my chest as we followed Maris down Forest Way. 'I know what a broken heart is,' I said to the kids. I had kept my emotions more or less in check during the service. I needed a release. 'Fucking bloody hell,' I said through tears and running nose.

'Fucking bloody hell,' Angela repeated. The other kids joined in.

'Fucking bloody hell!' we shouted, all the way to the cemetery, indifferent to the sensitivities of the occupants of other cars.

We could not stop our hoots of laughter. They cleared the head as we bent over and rocked, pressed hands to our faces, turned red and spluttered. Why were we laughing? It wasn't funny at all.

'No way to behave at a funeral,' someone recovered enough to say.

'Who cares? Fucking bloody hell.'

We composed ourselves by the time we arrived at the cemetery. Again we farewelled Maris. I threw a flower into the grave. Through my tears the words flowed. I can't remember exactly what I said. I remember the feelings — sadness, regret and guilt. I was up to my neck in grief. I thanked Maris for the life we had lived together but added, 'You shouldn't be here, Maris. You should be home, getting dinner ready.'

The family embraced and huddled like the Sydney Swans

before the ball bounce. Chris gave me the cross from Maris' coffin. That would be part of the shrine along with the candle.

Back at the church afternoon tea was still in progress. It was as if I was a guest of honour, a notoriety I would have swapped for anything. Things were hazy. A succession of people spoke to me. Most talked about Maris and what a wonderful person she was. One parishioner hoped that what happened to me would never happen to him. That was one comment I didn't need. It made me feel like an inferior being. Many people are confronted by death, particularly sudden death and wonder how they would cope. I remember discussing the Sydney Swans 2004 season. Besides Maris and me, a number of passionate Swans followers attend our church. We used to analyse each game and joke that once the football season was over we had nothing to talk about. We returned home where there was quite a crowd. The conversation was comparatively light-hearted.

'Thank you,' I said to Janne, 'for your wonderful tribute.'

'The music nearly broke me up, but I managed.'

We talked about sardines.

'I'm never going to eat another,' I said.

'Actually, I quite like them,' Janne replied.

As she was leaving, I said to her.

'Janne, I have a gift for you.'

She eyed me warily.

'What is it?'

'Six tins of sardines.'

Melissa was wonderful. She had only met Maris and the Sydney branch of the family on Friday, which would have been scary at any time, but the next day she was thrown into a family in deep crisis. Another girl of less maturity and character would have been overwhelmed. But not her. She threw herself into all the jobs and helped the girls with meal preparation, minding the grandchildren and keeping them busy. I said to Tim, 'Don't let this one go.'

'I don't intend to, Dad.'

Tim did a great job, too, with all the practical tasks — picking up people from the airport, attending to errands for the girls, assisting with shopping. He often put his arms around me, particularly when he saw me distressed and said, 'I love you, Dad.'

* * *

In retrospect, it is impossible to underestimate the importance of the funeral, a place of public ritual. So many friends were present, prepared to immerse themselves in the rituals of mourning. We did not have to face our loss alone. It was inspiring to be involved in the selection of prayers and songs. I did not want a cold, passionless, impersonal funeral full of dull prayers and platitudes. I wanted an inspiring tribute to Maris, recognising her for the person she was. It gave us, the family in shock, the opportunity to tell her story, express our love and her magnificent contribution to our family and the world. We gained an immeasurable amount of support. Our loss was acknowledged. The funeral was a most fitting farewell, a very sad occasion, but full of passion, inspiring us for the long, long harrowing journey ahead.

CHAPTER 7

Dear Noel and family,
What a moving experience it was to be at the Funeral
Mass for Maris. The wonderful tributes paid to her, and
Noel, your profound explanation of the depression Maris
suffered from, and the nature of the illness. Maris meant
so much to so many people, myself included. I shall
never forget the care and compassion she extended to
one of my friends who became quite difficult while she
was at Wesley Gardens Nursing Home. Nothing was
too much trouble for Maris. I shall not forget the night
Maris came around after Paul died to comfort us and to
bring a casserole for the family. May God comfort and
support you, and may you continue to rejoice in Maris'
wonderful life, and her commitment to other people in
spite of her depression.
Margaret and Merve

Friday morning. The first day of my life — without Maris. The funeral was over and it was now time to think about the wedding, the first family celebration without Maris. It was happening so soon, leaving no time for sorrow as practical matters were foremost.

I received a message from Anthea's father. Would I be wearing a dinner suit? His wife Margaret had insisted he dress up for this first wedding of their daughters. I said yes. I don't think that pleased Ron. I liked Ron. So did Maris. He reminded her of her father, a knockabout country man with a laconic sense of humour. In other circumstances, Maris would have attended to my dinner suit and made sure the dress shirt was washed and pressed and a tie was available. She would have laid them out on the bed. First question: where was my dinner suit? I hadn't seen it for ages. I found it at the back of the wardrobe, dusty but okay after a brush. Next question: what about a shirt? I found that, too. Maris washed it after the last occasion and hung it in the wardrobe. It needed a press. As I did the ironing when Maris was on evening shift, that presented no problem. I'm a slow ironer because I iron in front of the television, except when watching the Sydney Swans. They require my full concentration.

Back came a message from Ron. He was wearing a lounge suit. I was pleased, I'm afraid to say. I would not have to dress up. We all slipped into automatic again as we prepared for the wedding. I had not even thought about a gift. That would have been Maris' job. On such occasions she would decide and tell me, and I would agree and pay. I talked to Stephen and Anthea. Anthea's parents had paid for their New Zealand honeymoon package which included air fare, accommodation and car hire but they had no spending money as they had spent what little money they earned at Perisher on their wedding and on air fares for the USA where they were planning to work a season at the Utah ski fields. I thought of giving them $500.00 but I heard Maris' voice, 'Be generous, Noel.'

I was not deaf to her point so I gave them $1,000. Anthea's parents were paying for the reception. I said I would pay for the drinks.

That night we gathered for dinner at Angela's, exactly one week after our last gathering with Maris. We had a family conference, Angela and Guy, Jacinta and Rick, Tim and Melissa, my sister Maria and husband Joe, their daughter Annie, my brother Tom and his wife Robyn. Stephen and Anthea had left to attend to some last minute details.

'We have to think hard about tomorrow,' I said. 'We have to reach agreement on our attitude. We could be falling all over the place (one of Maris' favourite sayings) and look utterly miserable, or we could conceal our sadness and ensure that Anthea's family and friends enjoy themselves. They will be apprehensive, wondering what our mob's attitude might be. We have to make them feel comfortable. We want Stephen and Anthea to have a wonderful day.'

It was turning into an extraordinary year. Our family had seen the full circle of life — birth, death and marriage. Brody was born in August in Sydney. Jacinta had met Rick on the snow fields of Idaho where she had spent three winters working. After returning from America in our spring 2003, Jacinta fretted for Rick. She went back in October. Shortly after, Jacinta was pregnant. Maris' joke was that they were so overjoyed at seeing each other, they forgot to take the usual precautions. However, they were pleased and decided to marry. Jacinta wanted the baby born in Australia. They returned in June. It was a joyous event, Brody's birth. I have fond memories of Maris, the grandmother, nursing him, love and care written all over her face, a temporary respite from the ravages of her depression.

It could have been a joyful time. Jacinta came home with her baby, full of anxiety and love for her newborn. A newborn in the home is a wonderful experience. Birth is a miracle. To see a tiny healthy creature, complete with all its fingers, toes, eyes, ears and hair fills one with hope and thanks. What does the future hold for this innocent? you ask as you watch the routines of feeding, clothing and bathing. Jacinta loved her baby so much that I think she was sometimes reluctant to share him with others. But I was allowed as the grandfather to nurse him from time to time. I felt privileged.

Maris nursed him, too. She was experienced. She had raised four children and had received midwifery training. I remember during our courting days visiting her in working hours and admiring her skill in the nursery, carrying three, sometimes four, babies at the one time. She offered advice and reassured Jacinta that everything that Brody was doing was absolutely normal.

So the count for the year was one marriage, one birth, one death, and now another marriage. It reminded me of the popular film *Four Weddings and a Funeral*, except that our script was real and based on life.

CHAPTER 8

Dear Noel,
Words cannot express the sadness we all feel at the loss
of beautiful Maris. Her farewell at St Anthony's was
beautiful and as she so rightly deserved. How blessed she
was, Noel, to have you as her partner in life — someone
so gentle, kind, loving and understanding who supported
her through her illness. Our memories will always be of
quiet, beautiful smiling Maris who is now with God.
Shirley and Ian

The weather was warm and humid on Saturday November 6th, much the same as the previous Saturday. The same fractured sunlight shone through the bedroom window, but it shone on to a completely different life.

During the morning, I relived the events of the previous Saturday. In my mind's eye, I saw all the detail, Maris rocking on the bed, her driving down the lane, the arrival of the police, the trip to the hospital, the endless waiting, the room with Maris' body, the social worker in the corner. I endured the same anxiety and terror, as I was to suffer for many following Saturdays. Saturday was to become the worst day of the week.

I would be lying if I said I was looking forward to the wedding. I wanted to stay home, to be alone and to cry over my Maris. If I had decided to miss the wedding, people might have understood why, but I decided I had to follow the advice I gave to the family. This time I had to put on a brave front. I knew that the girls, Angela and Jacinta, would be determined to look as if they were enjoying themselves, despite what they felt, and make sure that everyone enjoyed themselves, too. We would support each other in upholding the family honour.

The wedding took place at Trinity Chapel, Macquarie University. The chapel has a very pleasant ambience. The surrounding eucalyptus trees create a bushland setting, a great background for the photographs. Anthea and Stephen were very involved in the community of students who frequented the chapel. In fact, she had worked part time for the church while she was undertaking her theology studies. The chapel was full.

As soon as I entered I placed Maris' candle on the altar as a symbol of her presence. The photographer was hovering around.

'Could you include a few shots of the candle?' I whispered to her as I walked back to my seat in the front row.

Stephen and Anthea were beautiful. I watched them with a mix of emotions as they went through the ritual of the ceremony. My heart was pounding with both sadness and joy; sad that my Maris wasn't here, joyful to see them so immersed in each other. The hard work she had put into her son was bearing fruit. I looked around at the other guests and everyone seemed to have a partner. I was acutely aware that I was on my own. I wiped a tear away before it ran down my cheek.

'You'd better get used to this, mate,' I said to myself. 'Save the tears for later and join in.'

I knew what Maris would have done. She would have forced herself to ignore her depression and present a calm and serene nature, listening, supporting, and making others feel comfortable, despite the anguish and turmoil inside. I needed to do the same. So I forced myself to chat to Anthea's parents and the other guests, congratulated the happy couple, participated in the photos as required, took a few photos myself, and generally did all the things that a father of the groom should.

I felt light-headed, detached, as if I wasn't really there. It seemed so unreal. I had buried my wife two days before and there I was, trying to be jolly. I just wanted to hide and weep.

The reception was held in North Sydney. The reception centre fronted a courtyard dominated by an enormous fig tree which somehow had survived the relentless high rise development. The cocktail party format worked. The atmosphere was relaxed and casual. There was plenty to eat and the platters kept coming. There was plenty to drink. I told the bar manager I would pay the bar account. The evening was light-hearted rather than wild or hilarious. People mixed very well, I'm happy to say. I drifted from group to group and met many of Anthea's friends and family.

But the small talk almost undid me. I was distracted, drifting back into myself, and, sometimes, I lost the thread of what was being said. Sometimes I had to guess what the other had just said and make a relevant comment. I hoped I got it right. Somehow, I managed. I wished Maris was with me. She was an expert with small talk and an excellent listener. She remembered names. She was able to put people at ease.

After the bridal waltz several couples joined in. I wished I was there, too, dancing with Maris. Thankfully no one asked me to dance. I was content to watch and quietly drink a beer.

I made a speech. I was scared, because I was so distracted, that I would slip and refer to the happy couple as Stephen and Danielle. I kept repeating to myself 'Stephen and Anthea, Stephen and Anthea' to try to break up the old habit. The girls said that the clanger dropped once only but didn't think anyone noticed.

I felt very proud of Stephen as he made his speech. Maris would have been proud, too, as she watched her Stephen, the one among our children who caused her the most concern. From a small child he had always marched to a different drum and been a puzzle to Maris, his teachers, sports coaches, our friends, but here he was, the mature young man, pledging his love and commitment to beautiful Anthea.

Among the guests was my brother-in-law, Ron, the husband of Catherine, Maris' sister, the first of the girls to suicide. Later in the evening, we talked. By that time, I had lost count of the number of beers I'd drunk, and I'm sure Ron had lost count of his bourbons.

'Maris was very good to me after Cath's death,' Ron began as we were offered another beer and bourbon. 'She was very supportive and non-judgemental. She didn't blame me at all. Not like some of my own family. They distanced themselves from me as if they thought I was to blame. Maris never did that.'

'I think Maris could understand some of the pain that Cath was going through,' I said.

'When I told the family the news of Maris' death, the third of the three sisters to suicide,' Ron continued, 'they were astounded. Maris was such a calm, kind person. I felt that some of their reserve had lifted as if they had arrived at a new understanding. Not one had died, but three.'

'Perhaps they realised there were factors contributing to their illness other than the relationships with their husbands.'

'I'd tried to explain this to my family after Cath died but my message fell on stony ground.'

'I don't suppose they knew Cath's, Loretta's and Maris' parents were nervy people and they were on medication for anxiety. One of the aunts was drowned in the Yarra. They suspected that was suicide. One of the uncles in the generation before died, too.' I'd finished another beer.

'I have to tell you, Noel, that when I first heard of Maris' death, I said to myself "Ah, I told you so!"'

'I'm glad that your family might have a better understanding. It's a tiny solace for me, Ron, but I'm pleased that one outcome of Maris dying is a reconciliation with your family.'

'Frank's not here tonight?' asked Ron. Frank was the husband of Loretta. She died in 2003.

'No, he couldn't come. I tried to get a message to him about Maris, but he must be away.'

Both Ron and Frank had gone through what I was now experiencing — massive guilt and striving to comprehend the incomprehensible. Ron was further along the road to recovery. As a senior executive, he had thrown himself into his corporate life. He had not remarried but had formed another relationship.

Frank was still going through the mill. I did not mention to Ron that Frank rang Maris frequently and had long conversations. He wanted to talk in great detail and Maris found the task of digging deep a strain. She did what she could to support him but she was drained of her limited resources as she was so vulnerable and needed all her depleted positive energy for herself.

'I'm very happy the wedding's gone so well. Everyone's enjoyed themselves,' I said to Angela and Jacinta as we collected the wedding gifts to take home at the end of the evening. 'You girls have been impeccable. I'm very proud. You really made the other mob feel welcome. No morose sitting in the corner.'

'Oh, Dad, as if we didn't feel like it,' Angela said.

We held each other.

* * *

Sunday afternoon and the lounge room was full of people. Anthea and Stephen and the family crowded out the flowers, and we all helped to open presents. Jacinta, the practical one, wrote the type of gift on each of the cards so that Anthea would know what to be grateful for when she got around to writing the thank you letters.

As the paper was folded and stored away I realised I had been operating on two levels. On the surface, I was calmly attending to the details of the funeral to be followed immediately by the wedding as if nothing of significance had happened. I had been extending support to my family. They in turn supported me. This game of grieving can't be played alone. But we had made it!

Below the surface, I was numb with shock and disbelief. It was as if I had been looking at the last week through a sound-proofed window — no sound but in my head a voice that screamed, 'This can't be happening to me. But it is. Why didn't I do more to stop Maris? Why isn't she here now, enjoying the wedding, the chatter and the presents?'

All around, people have been carrying on their normal lives as couples but mine had come to a deadening halt. My life had fallen apart and now I faced the long slow job of starting again and putting the broken pieces back together.

That journey had now begun.

CHAPTER 9

Dear Noel,
It would be hard to find anyone more genuine and caring than Maris — she will be remembered for her gentle, quiet nature and selfless concern for others. She tried so hard to overcome her own great fears and no one could have been more understanding and supportive than you Noel. Maris will be greatly missed by your family and her many friends. She richly deserved the huge send-off at Terrey Hills.
Jan and Michael

Dear Noel
I just wanted to let you know how deeply saddened I was to hear of Maris' sudden death. One cannot begin to imagine the deep shock and loss that you and your family are experiencing at the moment. I was pleased to see the weather was O.K. yesterday for the wedding. I hope it went ahead without too many problems. Hope to see you back at Lifeline when you are ready.
Ceiny

'Dad, there something's wrong with Vetbill. She's broken her hind legs, I think. The birds are attacking her.'

Vetbill is our cat. Originally she belonged to Stephen and Danielle. After their break-up they divided their goods. Stephen got the cat, Danielle took everything else. He brought Vetbill with him when he returned to live with us and left her when he moved out.

I found the family outside surrounding Vetbill. She could not move her hind legs. She looked at us plaintively as if pleading to know what was wrong.

'I know what's up,' I said.

Almost twelve months to the day, Vetbill acquired a tick. November is a bad month and our front garden is full of them. We took her to the local vet and five days later she came home with a bill for $500. After that we tried to keep Vetbill out of the front garden. Whenever Maris gardened there, she wanted to follow, so Maris locked her in the house. Vetbill had been neglected in the last week. She was missing Maris, too.

'She's got a tick.' I picked her up. 'Her legs aren't broken. They're paralysed.'

Jacinta and Rick took her to the vet. Sure enough he found a tick at the back of her neck, in the exact spot as before. Vetbill spent another five days in the animal hospital.

I'm not sure how we would have handled the situation if Vetbill had died. We were on the edge and her death might have tipped us over. That cat is still with me. Even as I type this, she is sleeping by my feet.

I was thankful that the media did not find out about Maris' death. I imagined the headline: *Woman falls to her death from Chatswood car park roof.* We were undergoing enough stress without having to deal with some tactless, pimply reporter sharpening her inquisitorial teeth.

I received a letter from the Coroner's Court explaining that the coroner had directed a post-mortem examination be undertaken. I was hoping that the coroner would not order full court procedures. The coroner's letter mentioned that the Department of Forensic Medicine provided a counselling service. I received a letter from the Department offering assistance. There was no time limit and anyone of the family could seek counselling free of charge. They included information on common reactions to trauma. There was a lot to absorb so I put them aside for later detailed study.

I visited Maris' grave daily. I needed to talk to her. For forty-two years we had chatted about the events of our day. I needed that to continue.

Some may find it quaint to talk to someone who is dead and expect a reply. My belief in Maris is a matter of faith. Faith is not the acceptance of a point of view based on the facts. It is my interpretation of reality based on my experience and understanding of its meaning. Those who have gone before us are still with us, albeit in another form. That is one of the traditions of my faith and I was grateful for that. My life would be unconceivable without it. My faith sustains me and lets me work through my tragedy.

I discussed all my problems on these visits. After living with her for so long I had a fair idea of her attitudes and responses to any question I was likely to put to her. Sometimes she would give me a serve, just as she used to rebuke me when she reckoned I got things wrong. The distance from my home was three and a half kilometres. I walked, so as well as meeting emotional needs I was getting exercise. I varied my route. Sometimes I walked by the Glenrose Shopping Centre and did a little shopping. At other times I cut across Frenchs Forest Showgrounds. At the cemetery I sat on the nearby seat and talked. I often rebuked her. 'You shouldn't be here, Maris. You should be home now.'

Other times I would say, 'There's space for me in the grave. I'll join you,' but I could hear her saying, 'Not yet.'

I did a lot of thinking aloud on that seat, basking in the late spring sun, the wind rustling the surrounding trees, the birds flitting from bush to bush and filling the silence with their songs. Where do I go from here? What do other blokes do when faced with the loss of their spouse? Some drown themselves in grog. I could understand why but it's a very temporary relief. Some take to womanising through prostitutes or one night stands. But Maris is the only woman I had ever slept with. I couldn't imagine making love with anyone else.

As I sat by that grave I felt that there were endless days stretching out before me with the enormous task of facing a new life. Pain, grief and confusion were to be my constant companions. During our life together, I sometimes wondered how I would cope if I lost Maris. I would fearfully dismiss the thought as too terrible. Yet here I was. Where will I get the strength? Where will I find the personal resources to get me through the next few months or years or whatever? How will I accept what has happened and get my life back to normal? Hope had become a scarce commodity. I could put no time limit on my grief. I would never be cured, but expect to be in a perpetual state of recovery, like incurring a wound that never quite heals. The only way to get through grief is to experience it. I would have to find courage in my suffering, courage in the midst of my emptiness and loss. I would become a different person, not the one I was before Maris died. I would never be that person again.

I guess I knew that the material I needed to work with, strength, courage, persistence, tenacity, motivation, faith, intelligence, was already within me. I already possessed some resilience. Except that I had never experienced anything like this before. Any stresses that had happened before seemed insignificant. I had not only lost my wife, I had lost her by suicide. Nothing had prepared me for that. I would have to call on inner resources I never had to use before. I was venturing into the unknown.

I was overwhelmed by sad and conflicting thoughts but I knew a time would come eventually when the incessant waves of emotional turmoil would subside. The road to healing was going to be a long, tough and lonely one but I had not lost hope completely.

I made two more decisions. The first was to internalise some of Maris' attitudes. She had so many admirable qualities which I would like to list among my own. In particular, she was always thinking of the other person. She placed her self interest behind that of others, particularly of the family. I must admit I always tended to think of my own self interest. Could I not put my own aside in the way that Maris did? I would become a living memorial of her finer qualities.

My second decision was to renew my involvement in Lifeline. In fact, it was through a suicide that I became involved with Lifeline in the first place. In my work as a psychologist I had seen a young man for career guidance. There seemed nothing unusual in his background.

I administered some tests and had two sessions with him discussing his career future. There was no hint. A week later, he died. I was the last professional to have contact with him. In hindsight I detected some clues, but I had missed them. I remember my reaction — self-doubt, guilt at my lack of awareness, a sense of inadequacy, shame and embarrassment. That young man led me to Lifeline where I undertook the training in suicide intervention. If I could not save him, I might save others. The suicide of Maris' two sisters, Catherine and Loretta, also alerted me that the training might be needed one day closer to home, a possibility that I did my best to deny and suppress. However, despite my training and that I have spoken to many suicidal people, I could not save my Maris. Many Lifeline counsellors who have suffered a personal tragedy find dealing with people in crisis too difficult and confronting and have to resign. I hoped I had the strength to continue to reach out to people in need, to give them hope by renewing my own.

One Monday afternoon I gave blood. I had been a regular donor and saw no reason not to give again. Every three months the Red Cross mobile blood bank turned up at Forestville. I was over the upper age limit but I came armed with a doctor's certificate stating that I was fit to give blood. I first began giving blood because my iron levels were high, and although they were now normal I remained a donor. Now I had additional motivation. If I couldn't save Maris, perhaps my blood might save someone else.

Back home I cast my eye over Maris' clothing and cosmetics. She always took care of her appearance and over the years had bought some very nice outfits. Sadly she would often buy something quite expensive which she would say made her feel a little better, but she would feel guilty and take the item back despite my encouragement to keep it. I invited the women in the family to look over her stuff and to take anything they fancied. They took some cosmetics.

'What should I do with the rest?' I asked myself. 'Nothing. They can stay where they are. One of these days I'll remove them, donate them to Lifeline, and keep a few of my favourite garments, but for the time being...'

I looked into the drawer beside my bed. It contained many private things, including our aids for love making. I looked across the bed. Empty. We found fulfilment and a deep satisfaction in our sex life. I would never have sex with her again, and as I couldn't imagine having sex with anyone else, I tossed out all the paraphernalia — medication, lubricant, the lot.

* * *

Wednesday night saw the meeting of the Catenians. The Catenians is a Catholic Men's society which holds a monthly dinner meeting. I joined them about a year previously. My friend Bob, who is also a mechanic and services our cars, had been suggesting for years that I should come along one night. I kept forgetting the name. Then in my role as editor of the Terrey Graph, I received an advertisement for membership.

'Is this the mob you've been talking to me about?' I asked Bob.

'Sure is. Why don't you come along?' was his reply.

So I did and eventually went through their initiation and joined. Maris was pleased. She said I should get out and mix with other blokes more often as I had worked at home for some years and had no work colleagues.

My first impression of the Catenians was that they were old-fashioned, anachronistic and conservative. They didn't do anything, had no objectives other than fellowship and care for each other. They called each other Brother. I was indifferent and debated each month whether I should go. But Maris always encouraged me. I already knew a number of men from our own parish and was slowly getting to know the others. They were good blokes, friendly and welcoming. I was amazed to find them at the funeral. They formed a guard of honour as we drove out of the church grounds. This single act of support blew my mind away. It was so unexpected. It changed my attitudes to the Catenians.

So I wanted to attend the November meeting in order to thank the members but at the same time I struggled. It would be my first public appearance since...

I knew I had to get out and about. So I dressed in my suit, the only occasion those days for dressing up, and went to the meeting. I was very well received and many members offered their support. I gave a little speech of thanks and told the members how my attitude had changed. I enjoyed the company that night and resolved I would get along to meetings as often as I could.

Sundays I went to church. It was a trial.

'I don't think going to church is doing me any good,' I said to a friend, 'because I finish up crying every time.'

Maris and I went to church together every Sunday. Every Sunday we walked to the front to receive Communion. Now the most painful part of church was receiving Communion on my own. Even the music bought on tears, particularly if it was a piece sung at the funeral. People would note my distress and comfort me. Most upsetting for me was a Bereavement Mass held every year in November to remember the departed among the parish family. To see Maris' name on an overhead brought home the cruel reality.

I could have avoided these emotional situations and so avoid the anguish, but I needed to confront the pain then and there. If I didn't, it could emerge in unexpected ways. I needed to expose my pain to the light. We can be tempted to bury our painful emotions and pretend they are dead. But they live silently within in a shadow world that stirs within us.

Nothing heals in the dark.

CHAPTER 10

Dear Noel and family,
I had the privilege of knowing Sister Braun at Wesley
Gardens where I am still employed within the mainte-
nance section. Through her requests for maintenance I
came to know Sister Braun as a kind and loving RN
whose care for the elderly and frail was indicative of her
faith put into practice. At her funeral service I did not
approach you and introduce myself as I felt it would
have been an intrusion at a very poignant time.
Michael

I had some unfinished business. I bought the wallaby grass from the nursery but decided to delay
the gum tree because a tiny sapling had emerged
from the soil in roughly the spot we had in mind. I called it
Maris' tree.

Stephen and Anthea returned from their honeymoon, full
of stories of their experience. Stephen told me that when looking for souvenir gifts for the family, several times he thought
of items that would suit Mum but then had to remind himself. He gave me a beer mug.

Constable Catherine contacted me.

'The coroner requires more information. Would you come to Chatswood station and make a statement.

I wasn't keen on visiting Chatswood. I had to drive past Chatswood Chase car park to get to the police station. As I was feeling fragile, I asked Stephen and Anthea to accompany me.

The station was being rebuilt, so we went to temporary wooden offices in the Council car park for the 8 pm appointment. I deliberately looked the other way as we passed Chatswood Chase. Catherine was out on patrol and arrived late. She arrived, bristling with her gun and other patrol gear, as if ready to do battle with the worst of criminals. Her gear seemed incongruous with the gentle nature that she had shown me. Catherine started typing. My statement began. 'I knew Maris Braun for forty-five years; we were married for forty-one of those years,' I said.

A lifetime of living together summarised in fifteen austere words. What manner of life did we lead? Where was the richness, the joys, the sorrows, the struggles, the challenges, the victories, defeats, renewals? The new beginnings of a union that saw four children?

Catherine was patient. She managed to balance a sensitive concern with essential cross-questioning but it was evident she had other things to do. She should have been out on patrol, chasing burglars or quelling riots, instead of attending to this necessary paperwork and supporting an old widower. I read the statement and made two grammar corrections — a plural verb with a single subject, use of the indicative instead of the subjective. Catherine was annoyed. She printed the statement again.

'I'm sorry for keeping you away from catching bank robbers,'

I said, 'but if I am to sign a statement, I would prefer it to be grammatically correct as well as the truth.'

* * *

Life was slowly becoming less insane. I missed a few weeks attending the gym so I resumed my programme of running treadmills and pumping weights. The gym staff knew of Maris' death. But they worked me just as hard.

I did an afternoon shift with Lifeline. Donna was very encouraging. 'Noel, you're to stop if you find any calls too much to handle.'

'I reckon, Donna, that the best way to cope with this crisis in my own life is to help other people with their crises,' I told her.

As I took the phone calls and spoke to people with a wide range of issues, I wondered how I would cope with a suicidal call, but there were none that afternoon. I was pleased I handled the shift. I suppose that by that time I maintained a more-or-less professional approach. When I started at Lifeline I took the callers' problems home with me, but by then I was able to leave them behind. In fact, I was hard pressed to even remember the calls. I spoke with the Lifeline staff and other telephone counsellors on shift. They were very supportive. It felt good to be part of the Lifeline family again.

I resumed my work as an interviewer with the Australian Bureau of Statistics. I did so reluctantly as I was sick of it and had to crank myself up to tackle each month's work load. The Bureau offered an employee assistance programme to its employers. One night I was feeling low and I needed to talk to someone. Ringing Lifeline I thought was inappropriate, so I rang the assistance number. I was put on to a counsellor who broke every rule in the book about grief counselling. He talked about himself, spoke at length about his own father's death, wondered how he would react if a person close to him suicided, wondered if I would get any support from my church because of its attitude towards suicide. To say that I came off that call angry is an understatement. I was furious. After, I walked around the house banging doors.

Banks had to be contacted. I was used to N J & M C Braun on cheques and statements. It was a sadness to ask for Maris' name to be removed. Of our two banks, one was impersonal. The staff at the other were empathetic, commenting how difficult it must be to attend to this formal stuff.

I rang the lawyer who had our wills. Everything was in joint names, and our wills left everything to each other. The house was in joint names. There was no debt but the mortgage was still registered with the bank. If I wanted the house in my name, the mortgage would have to be unregistered. A fee was involved. I could delay that expense.

I had an appointment with my accountant to discuss the tax situation and the implications of Maris' death for my company structure. Maris and I were directors. I met our financial planning consultant. We arranged for Maris' allocated pension to be directed to me.

All these practical re-arrangements left me exhausted. Sometimes I wanted to hide, to shut out the world and protect myself. Sometimes, I felt quite rational and logical as I attended to these tasks. At other times, I felt anxious, confused and bewildered. My mind was shooting in all directions. I'd start a task and then forget what I was supposed to be doing and go off doing something else. I seemed to be plagued with a tension that made me restless and had me bouncing off walls. I had to concentrate in order to focus on completing the task. For a while I thought I was going senile or stupid. I tried to solve the problem by writing down a list of what I wanted to do and crossing them off as they were completed. It worked... sometimes.

I was very grateful for the support of my two daughters. Jacinta, Rick and Brody were still living with me. I was grateful for their racket in the house, which would have been very lonely, indeed, without them. Jacinta ran the household, did the cooking and cleaning, and attended to her baby, as well as keeping an eye on me. Angela had her own family of three children, but she rang me every other day. We had both received information from the Department of Forensic Medicine on grieving. We had a competition of upstaging each other as to which symptoms of grief we were experiencing that day.

Maris loved her grandchildren. I was conscious that they had lost their grandmother. Tessa painted a portrait of Gran. I framed it and hung it at the top of our stairs for me to see every time I went into the bedroom. I welcome the opportunity to do the child minding for Angela that Maris had done. I came to know my grandchildren better, a tiny benefit, I suppose, from Maris' death. At first, they didn't have much to say about Maris, but one afternoon I was playing a game with Eliza when she said, 'Gran died.'

Later, playing a ball game with Hugh, he said 'Gran died,' but added the detail 'from a bump on the head.'

One day I walked Eliza to the playground where we ran around the park and played on the equipment. She asked me many times, 'Why did Gran die?' I didn't have an answer.

What to tell young children must be a task that faces every bereaved family. One of these days we will have to explain everything. Perhaps they already know more than we realise.

In the meantime, I visited the cemetery and talked to Maris about all the arrangements I was making, admonishing her that I shouldn't be doing them and that she should be home. I told her the family news and, in particular, what the grandchildren were up to. I ensured the flowers were fresh and spurned the notion of plastic flowers. The weather was mostly fine and I walked the three and a half kilometres with cap and backpack, calling at the shopping centre either on the way or coming home. I used to enter the cemetery by the front gate, but I found a short cut through the bush which took off about 500 meters and avoided descending and ascending a hill.

'Dad, you should still take the long way,' Angela warned me on one of her calls, 'and get more exercise.'

The local bike shop was moving to another location and offered twenty per cent off all stock. If there was ever a time to buy a mountain bike, the time was then. So I sometimes rode the new bike to the cemetery. But I preferred to walk.

It occurred to me that I hadn't seen Gana and Hos. They were our neighbours at the front. Did they know? All the other neighbours knew because I had received their cards. As I walked down the sixty steps for the mail or the newspaper, I would often pause to chat if they were outside. Maris would often stop her gardening for a talk. So three weeks after her death, I braced myself and knocked on their door. They didn't know. They were stunned. Out poured the emotion in the full shock of first knowledge. I copped their blast, a mixture of grief and anger. They were cross I hadn't told them. I had to apologise again and again. Hos only said, 'What a waste!' Gana poured out a mixture of words and tears. I had to repeat the details several times. She was unable to take it in. I regressed three weeks to that terrible afternoon telling people of Maris' death and having to repeat myself to counter their disbelief. After that encounter, I needed a beer.

Stephen and Anthea eventually received their visas. Two days later they were on the plane for USA. I drove them to the airport. As I dropped them off, the tears flowed again. In the confusion of an airport drop off, cars banked up waiting for my spot, officials telling us to move on, I hugged them and thanked them for their support, in particular Anthea.

'I'm sorry for Maris that she stuffed up your wedding. You did a great thing, deciding to carry on.'

The people waiting were getting impatient but I was losing one of my children, albeit for six months, to the other side of the world.

I shed more tears in the month of November than any other month in my life. Grief wafted down every path and alleyway like an invisible cloud. It drifted into my lonely bed every night, wrapped itself around my dinner table, seeped under the door of my bathroom, settled on my computer, followed me to church and sneaked up from behind in most unexpected ways.

Jacinta, Rick and Brody were due to return to the States early January.

'Why not visit us?' Jacinta suggested. 'You could visit Stephen and Anthea, too.'

'Why not?' I said to Maris.

There are many threads running through our lives and gradually I was taking them up again.

One of these threads was my writing. I wrote the first draft of *Friend and Philosopher* about 30 years ago. It's a novel based on my experience as a teacher in one teacher schools. I put the manuscript aside for many years to attend to my career and raising a family with the intention that one day I would take it up again. That day was about six years prior. I wrote many drafts and continued to rewrite until I was satisfied that I had a readable product. Maris contributed greatly and was able to draw on her own experience as a country girl. She encouraged me to persevere. Writing a novel is a long, lonely job. She read the many drafts and made lots of suggestions.

One day I asked her, 'What's a nice name for a country lass?'

'Beth,' she replied.

So Beth was my main female character. I sent the manuscript to mainstream publishers and received the inevitable rejection slips. Eventually late in 2003 I was accepted by a small publisher who was sympathetic to new authors. The editing process took up the first half of 2004 and I received five copies of the galley prints in August. What a thrill to see my book in print! The designer did an excellent job of the cover. All those years of hard work had some point. Maris was very proud. I found out after she died that she had spoken to many people about the book.

About the middle of November the publisher contacted me with a copy of a review — a piece of good news in an otherwise bleak month. I decided to dedicate the book to Maris and donate the profits to Lifeline. The dedication read: *Dedicated to the memory of my cherished wife, Maris, whose continuing support, encouragement and quiet dedication made this book possible.* I supplied a photograph, the amputated one.

I attended a Time Out group meeting for November. The group met at St Anthony's on the second Friday morning and concerned themselves with meditation, reflection and prayer. It was for people who needed a little time out from their daily lives. Maris gained a lot from these meetings. This was where she shared some of her anguish with people who had their own pain. I had offered to go to these groups with her, but she said it was something she wanted to do on her own. I found the group very supportive and was able to share some of my anguish with understanding and supportive people.

* * *

November-December is hamper time at St Anthony's. Every year parishioners assemble Christmas hampers for people in need. Lists go up in November, giving details of families; ages and number of children. The people select a family and make up a hamper complete with gifts. Maris always selected a family with four children and ensured our children were involved with gift purchase. She spent lots of time in the supermarket selecting not only the basics, but nice toilet paper, serviettes or expensive toiletry items that a struggling family could not afford. So I selected a family with four children and trolled the supermarket for the items that Maris would have bought.

I met other parishioners in the supermarket. When I told them what I was doing, they wanted to help. They made suggestions on what to include. I packed four boxes of goods and gifts and wrapped them in Christmas paper, a tough job for me as gift wrapping is not one of my skills. It was Maris who made the packages look so neat. 'I've tried to do exactly the same as you, Maris,' I said when the job was finished. I hope the family that received my hampers experienced a similar joy.

I thought about my trip. Jacinta and Rick were leaving early January for Oregon so perhaps I could join them a month later. Why not visit some other places in USA as well? Why not keep on going to Europe? To London and Paris? Why not purchase an around-the-world trip? I had the time and only myself to organise. I visited a travel agent and, stage by stage, we worked out the itinerary.

When friends asked how I was going, I told them about my trip. They thought it was a good idea, a way of seeing me through these early stages of bereavement. I thought they were right, too. It was certainly a distraction because I spent a lot of time planning and organising accommodation via the internet.

One day, Jacinta spoke to me. 'I'd like Brody to be christened before we return to America. I'm sure it's something that Mum would have liked.'

'No worries, Cint.' I was very pleased.

'I'd like him baptised at St Anthony's because that was my church as a child,' she reasoned.

So on December 12th Father Brendan baptised Brody in the Catholic rite. Another family event without Maris.

'You better get used to this, mate,' I kept on reminding myself during the service. Afterwards, over a celebratory cup of tea, I asked Father Brendan, 'Do you have someone to be

Baby Jesus at the Christmas Mass?' It was the practice to hold a pageant of the Christmas story with a live baby Jesus, the parents being Mary and Joseph.

'Not yet.'

'I'm sure Brody would be great.'

* * *

Christmas cards began to arrive. Most were addressed to me, but a few were addressed to us both, mainly from Melbourne friends. I had to let them know.

I had my first session with Kate, from the Department of Forensic Medicine. I found her a good counsellor as well as a wise, warm and compassionate human being. She invited me to a post-suicide support group held every month. Angela saw her a few days later.

Christmas arrived in no time. My brother Tom and wife Robyn from Melbourne joined us. Tim could not join us as he could not get sufficient time off from work. The holiday period was a busy time for car hire. Stephen and Anthea were already in America. So to celebrate this first Christmas without Maris I had my brother, Angela and Jacinta and their families. We attended the children's Christmas Eve Mass at St Anthony's. Normally held outside to cater for the extra crowd in fine, balmy weather, the heavy downpour set in motion the wet weather programme and we squeezed inside. It was a jolly Mass. Brody was the centre of attention as baby Jesus with Jacinta and Rick dressed as Mary and Joseph. I was bursting with pride. Squashed into the church, I sat on the floor and had no hesitation in telling everyone around me that baby Jesus was my grandson. Jacinta entered into the spirit and enjoyed the occasion but Rick was self conscious, dressed as Joseph. He probably thought that this was another of those bizarre Australian customs. We referred to Brody as BJ (baby Jesus). How my heart ached for Maris to be with me to share my pride. She would have rebuked me for being so vocal.

Our collective recollections of our first Christmas without Maris are very blurred. I remember the celebrations were rowdy, with lots of laughter and loud conversations.

Perhaps, as a family we were still numb with shock but we forced ourselves to be jolly.

The day after Christmas saw the tsunami in South East Asia, a disaster of catastrophic proportions. It put my own personal tragedy in a new light to see television images of men crying uncontrollably over the loss of their families. For each man's grief depicted, there were thousands of survivors similarly distraught. I cried with them as I remembered my own loss. Life is transient, whimsical, capricious and arbitrary. Up to that time, my life was concentrating on coping with my loss. Now a new reality, something outside my frame of reference, had leapt into my world and rearranged it. Dreadful as the tsunami was, the immensity of its destruction and human suffering made me place my grief over Maris' death into a new perspective. I still felt the pain just as intensely, but it gave me another view and dragged me away from self absorption.

We celebrated New Year's Eve. Maris and I usually spent it quietly and never bothered with the harbourside celebrations. However, we had been invited by brother-in-law Ron to his apartment at Edgecliff to watch the fireworks. We started the evening at Angela's with a few drinks and nibbles. Jacinta,

Rick and I drove to Artarmon and caught the train to Edge-cliff — the first time I had been on a train on New Year's Eve. Our fellow passengers were good humoured, rules about consuming alcohol on trains treated with disdain. The train trip back after the fireworks was equally happy. Our fellow passengers were a group of chatty friendly young men. I'd had a few drinks during the evening, I'm afraid, so I found myself engaging them in lots of banter. They called me the professor. Jacinta and Rick reckoned that in addition to alcohol they were on drugs. Perhaps they were, but to me they were just youthfully high-spirited, another reminder of the zest for life that Maris chose to forfeit.

So ended 2004, a bad year, the worst of years.

CHAPTER 11

For Christmas I have four wishes.
The first is for my two front teeth.
The second is that my Gran did not die so my mum
could be happy.
The third is that Santa will bring me a Baby miracle.
My final wish is for all the poor people in the world to
have some presents from Santa.
Tessa

The start of the new year saw Jacinta, Rick and Brody returning to the USA. I was on my own in my five bedroom house. I was busy interviewing for the Australian Bureau of Statistics and planning my trip. I accepted invitations to dinner. I did my first overnight shift for Lifeline. I had one suicide-in-progress call but I handled it and put aside my own emotions to deal with the caller's crisis.

By mid January I reckoned I had received all the cards and letters I was going to receive. I needed to reply. People usually send printed cards. The message is brief and often a prayer is included. But everyone receives the same reply. If I had died, Maris would have hand written a personal letter to everyone. I looked for suitable stationery and bought the local shopping centre stock of a writing pad with the message — *Keep your eyes open and your spirit dancing*, with a silhouette of a dancing figure. I commenced the job of writing hundreds of letters. It was a task I wanted to do. It kept me busy. I needed to be.

One unusually cool morning while driving, I heard a news items on the ABC that there had been a fatal massive avalanche at Park City, Utah. My ears pricked up. That was where Stephen was. While working at Perisher he went cross country skiing in the back country. Jacinta had given him lots of warnings not to do the same in America as the country would be unfamiliar. I did not want to lose another family member. I rang Jacinta in Oregon.

'We haven't heard any news here,' she said, 'but I'll ring Park City.'

'It sounded pretty bad, Cint.'

'Sit tight, Dad. I'll call you back.'

I felt those old, familiar troops begin to march back into my stomach. When the phone rang again, I pounced.

It was Jacinta. 'I've spoken to Stephen's supervisor on the mountain. He says he's seen Stephen this morning. I asked him to get Stephen to ring his Dad when he finishes work.'

It's hard to describe how thankful I was to hear her reassurance coming from the other side of the world.

'It sounds as if Stephen hasn't come to any harm.'

A few hours later, Stephen rang.

'I'm still alive, Dad,' he said in his laconic, laid back voice. 'The avalanche was large but in a canyon which is known as dangerous and where nobody except the foolhardy would venture.'

I was relieved to hear his voice. I was fragile. It didn't take much to panic me when the family's safety was involved.

I had heard that Brenda and Graeme were in Sydney. They had a house in Forestville but they had one in London, too. Maris and I had stayed with them in London. I invited them to dinner. I met Patricia in the supermarket where I was shopping for the dinner. I had just bought some chicken and beef kebabs. Patricia knew them well.

'They're a nightmare to feed,' she exclaimed. 'Brenda's a vegetarian and Graeme never eats chicken.'

I was nervous as this was my first dinner party without Maris. I need not have worried. Brenda and Graeme ate the kebabs and helped themselves to extras. I told them about my impending trip and Brenda insisted I stay with them in London. She had been into many things over the years. At that time she was into philosophy and she gave me a copy of *The Power of Now* by Eckhart Tolle.

I took a quick trip to Melbourne to say goodbye to family, my son Tim and my brother Tom. The short trip reflected my restlessness and the tension which seems to invade my body regularly, which I still experience as I write this. Maris' death was turning me into a nomad and vagabond, unable to settle anywhere for long without feeling agitated and needing to move on. While in Melbourne I spoke to the publisher. The editing process was complete. It only remained for me to check the final proof before printing an initial 1000 copies in Hong Kong. The proof was on its way, he said. He would send it on to Sydney. I suggested it would arrive after I departed. Rather than wait until I returned to Australia, I gave him the address of Rick's parents in Oregon.

Chapter 12

Dear Noel
I will miss Maris' weekly visit to have her hair done. We
always talked about our families trying to solve their
problems. Little did I know Maris had a big problem
herself, I am so sorry I missed seeing this. I was glad I
made the service. It was a beautiful Mass. She would
have been proud of you all, she often talked about
that.
Dianne

As I was packing for my trip, I realised that I had
made another decision, another choice, almost
subconsciously. I could have succumbed to
despondency and despair and been destroyed by Maris' death.
My despair could have spread to the family and destroyed
them. But I had chosen to go on living and to value each
moment in a way that I never did before.

I decided I would value every moment of my trip and be
open to every event and to every person I met. I would be
aware that it isn't the places you visit but the people you meet
there that is the vital experience. Nevertheless, it was bizarre
to prepare for a trip on my own. I had travelled overseas a

number of times but on every occasion I had a companion, initially with my work colleagues to USA, but more recently with Maris.

Together we had visited Japan, Ireland, the United Kingdom and joined a pilgrimage through Turkey, Greece and Italy. We discussed every stage of our planning. Maris would discover an item of interest in the travel section of the newspaper and show it to me. We would discuss when to go and what to take. Maris was inclined to pack everything 'just in case.' I was more inclined to travel light.

I looked at my things. What would she say now? She'd probably say, 'Noel, it might be cold. You might just need that blue jumper.' I put it in my case.

February 3rd 2005 saw me flying high over the Pacific still with most of the cards. I spent the time writing letters. The security screening at San Francisco was a nightmare, but it was also comical — lots of large, black security people huge with authority, shouting at intimidated shoeless travellers. 'Who put that stroller here?' screamed one very large black man to a tiny lady holding a baby.

I spent the time waiting for the connecting flight to Crescent City writing more letters. Crescent City airport was not much more than a tin shed. Jacinta, Rick and Brody were at the airport to meet me. Brookings was a short distance over the state border in Oregon. The house was out of town and sat on a hill overlooking the Pacific Ocean. Over a beautiful meal of beef spare ribs and two bottles of Australian wine, purchased at the local supermarket, we spent the evening chatting.

I had thought by now that America would be asphalted over, but here I was witness to a wilderness that rolled down

to the ocean. I walked through Redwood forests, along beautifully rugged ocean beaches. I attended the local Lutheran
church. I had dinner with friends. In between, I wrote more
letters which I sent back to Angela to post in Australia.

Among the people I met were Jean and Gail. They were
friends of Barbara, visiting from San Francisco. They were
interested in me as a writer. Being Australian also made me
a novelty. Jacinta told me later they found me 'charming'.
As I chatted with these two exuberant women, I recalled a
remark made by Kate, my counsellor. I was now a very eligible bachelor. This I could not imagine. Chasing women
was not on my mind.

I had fatherly chats with Jacinta about her uncertain
future as we walked along quiet beach tracks with Brody in
a backpack. She was missing home. She was missing a mum
to talk to, which made me aware I had to be available when
my children needed me.

Jacinta was keen to show me something of her life in
America. We left behind the beautiful coastal forests and
drove through Oregon to Portland where I met more of
Rick's family.

We drove on to Idaho. Jacinta and Rick worked at the Sun
Valley ski resort and lived in Ketchum. Our destination was
Fairfield, an hour short of Ketchum. Jacinta's friend Karen
had offered us her weekender. The house was well insulated
and built to hold in all the heat through a Finnish design
fire box. It was frozen in time, full of toys and paintings of a
pre-schooler. Outside was a world of snow. The wide prairies
and the surrounding hills and mountains were covered in
white. Nearby was Soldier Mountain, an undeveloped ski run
with one snow lift. The house became our base for visiting

Ketchum and Sun Valley. Jacinta and Rick were nostalgic. They met, lived and worked here. Rick wanted to live here again but Jacinta was ambivalent whether to call America home.

I met their many friends. We visited their old drinking spots such as Lefty's, Whiskey Jacques and Grumpy's. We spent President's Day, a public holiday for the birthdays of George Washington and Abraham Lincoln, on Soldier Mountain.

In this beautiful white wilderness, I finished the job of replying to the condolence letters. Time to start the post cards. Maris used to write them and now I was doing her job. There were so many I wanted to send to family, to friends and others whom I knew had my interests at heart.

Karen had posted many one liner inspirational messages around the house. I enjoyed reading them. One in particular was a grace before meals: *In this food I see clearly the presence of the entire universe supporting my existence.* These messages inspired me. I created a slogan for myself, a resolution for my new life. Meet my challenges with C's rather than S's. C stood for Confidence, Courage, Conviction, Curiosity, Compassion. S stood for Safety, Security or Social Approval. I should be ready to challenge myself, to step out beyond my boundaries, of my comfort zone. I should not be too concerned about security or what people thought about my actions. I told Jacinta and Rick of my slogan. They added their own C's and S's. I was to remind myself often of my C's and S's.

I was getting toey about the time I would be on my own. Up to now I had been with Jacinta and in a few days I would be with Stephen and then...

This trip was akin to a bridge between my former life with Maris and a life on my own. I was in transition. I had chosen to continue living. I was in the process of re-defining myself, of finding a new identity. I could not go back. It was essential I go on.

After ten days in Idaho we drove to Utah, to Park City, piled high with snow. We had difficulty finding Stephen and Anthea's apartment among a forest of apartment buildings. I rang him on the mobile and I heard his familiar and distinctive thumping down the stairs but in another building to the one I thought was his. I slipped on the iced sidewalk and fell heavily on my hip. I broke nothing but had a bruise and a sore hip for weeks. Lucky I was wearing a thick padded jacket. I found my spectacles under a car. I thanked God I did not sustain an injury, here in America where, I'm told, hospital and medicals bill can send a millionaire broke. Maris was looking after me.

I met Stephen and Anthea's flatmates — four young Australians and one set of parents who were staying too, so nine people were squeezed into the three bedrooms. The place was a squat, the only furniture being a couch and television. Everyone slept on the floor. Stephen and Anthea gave up their mattress to me and they slept on the floor during my two-night visit. They had a balcony which gave a view over Park City. Long icicles hung from the guttering. Stephen touched one and it broke off with a whoosh. A slender deadly javelin fell three stories to the ground. Fortunately no one was standing below.

I had received an email from my publisher that my proofs were ready. I had asked for them to be sent to Stephen's address but they had not arrived. I realised that I had forgotten to include the unit number in the address. I checked the local post office and there they were, waiting for me to turn up. Those proofs had travelled around the world, from Hong Kong, Sydney, Oregon, and now Utah. I like to think Maris guided them to me.

I left Stephen and Anthea the next day. I was dropped at the airport in Salt Lake City and while waiting began to read every word of the proofs.

My next stop was Washington DC. I took the plane to Denver then to Baltimore, reading those proofs all the way. I arrived quite late with the time changes. I had planned to use public transport everywhere but as it was late so I took a taxi to the youth hostel. My taxi driver was pleasant. He talked the whole trip then charged me $80.00. No wonder he was so chirpy.

After booking into the hostel, I went looking for a place to eat. I could hear Maris saying, 'Be careful. This is America, you know.' I wasn't sure whether Washington was safe to walk around at night, but apart from the beggars, no one bothered me. One beggar recognised my accent and was keen to tell how he loved the Australians he met during his service in Vietnam. He was such a charmer I just had to give him money. I found a McDonalds three blocks away. I ate about midnight. My fellow diners were people just finishing work. One was keen to tell me the troubles he'd had that night. Back in my room I stayed up late to finish checking the proofs.

Next morning I wanted to send an email to the publisher to say the proofs were okay. The Hostel's computers were not functioning. Try the public library, I was told. To use their computers I had to join the Martin Luther King Junior Memorial Library. I'm probably still a member.

Then began my three days touring Washington. It was very, very cold, colder than the mountains of Utah. The sky was cloudless, the keen wind pierced my ears. Maris would have hated it. She would have stayed in the warmth of the hostel. I visited all the national buildings and museums. The highlight was the Arlington Cemetery where I saw the graves of John F and Robert Kennedy. I was quite moved and thought about Maris and her struggle. I felt her presence besides me as I walked around the undulating hills of the cemetery, drifts of snow everywhere.

Washington was fascinating. Among impressive buildings, monuments and symbols of American national pride were hundreds of beggars. At night they seemed to sleep wherever they could. Around the hostel were numerous squats of people wrapped up in all manner of clothing against the cold. One night I passed a group huddled in a stairway. I heard one voice say, 'Come on, man, let's get out and make some money.'

People asked me for directions. An older man on his own, perhaps I looked like a local. Before I left Australia, Angela had offered me plenty of warnings including, 'Blend in, Dad, blend in!' I was following her advice successfully. Being on your own has its disadvantages. You have no one to share your spontaneous impressions, but you talk to others and others talk to you. At the hostel, I chatted with a number of my fellow guests: Dillon from Canberra, Paul from London who had been to Australia, Lucy from New Zealand, some American teenagers from Gettysburg, and many others whose names I did not record. I found the shop assistants friendly and helpful. A lady at the post office asked me how many grandchildren I had. She gave me four free colouring books.

I was annoyed with myself that I had used a taxi to get to the hostel. I took the Metro and a bus to Dulles Airport for New York. On the short plane trip, I sat next to Pat while her two friends sat together. They were going to a conference and were discussing the agenda. Pat wasn't going to any conference. She had come for the ride and to shop. She asked me questions and was impressed by my writing. I told her something of my story and about my C's and S's. She wrote them down. At JFK airport I caught the air train but went around and around the circuit until I worked out how to get out at Station D where I caught the subway to 96th Street.

The hostel was old and cramped with narrow stairways. My room was on the third floor and it took an effort to get my case up the stairs. The room was supposed to be for two, but there was barely enough space for one. If Maris had been with me, we would have been falling over each other. The common area and the kitchen were hopelessly inadequate. What a contrast to the Washington hostel! I hoped there would be no emergencies during my stay. I tried the kitchen to make a cup of tea and found a group of French speaking Belgians had squeezed in and were eating spaghetti.

I had always wanted to attend a concert at world famous Carnegie Hall, so the next day I visited Carnegie Hall and bought a ticket. I took the subway to Times Square. Wow! To see Times Square for the first time was amazing. I wanted to see a Broadway show. From the dozens available I picked *Fiddler on the Roof*. I had a look around Central Park. It was covered in snow. There was more to see at Grand Central Station, which reminded me of a few old film settings. That evening I ate at the Kinsdale Tavern, an Irish pub. In the bar were seven TVs each with a different program. Add to that the shouting over the cacophony and you have a microcosm of New York. Someone turned on the jukebox and played AC/DC *If you want blood, you've got it.* Back at the hostel the Belgians were having another meal of spaghetti. 'C'est moins cher,' (It's cheap), one laughed. Three Japanese girls wanted to go out for something to eat but were scared of the streets. I walked them to the Kinsdale Tavern.

The following day's forecast was for snow and winds. I left the hostel and walked to the subway. On every subway trip I made in New York City, a man would appear in the carriage and beg for money with a story of his life. This trip was no exception. This man said he was a Vietnam veteran, had AIDS, and was cold and hungry. On other trips buskers played musical instruments. One fellow put on a puppet show. People were continually walking through from carriage to carriage. I was told that the passengers stared straight ahead and made no eye contact. But they did. They talked to each other. There seemed to be a camaraderie among the regulars. The carriages were dirty and most badly needed refurbishment. The stations were filthy but the trains were regular.

I got off the train at Wall Street and made my way to Ground Zero. They had spread salt on the road and sidewalks in anticipation of the snow which was starting to fall heavily. Seeing the lists of all the people who had died on September Eleven was moving. I was impressed by the models of what they planned to build in place of the World Trade Centre. But it was getting so cold I sought shelter in St Paul's Chapel in the shadow of the Twin Towers. How it escaped when the towers collapsed is beyond me. It dates from colonial days and there was a stall where George Washington worshiped when the seat of federal government was still in New York. Around the walls were displays depicting the support the congregation played post September 11. I felt proud of that group. Our people back at Terrey Hills would have done exactly the same. That day they were conducting auditions for future concerts. I heard Mozart and Chopin played by a pianist and a flute trio and thought of my parishioners back at St Anthony's.

It was a struggle getting back to the hostel through the wind, snow and ice. I helped a lady stuck in an iced gutter with a pram. I was careful on the icy sidewalks. I didn't want another fall.

I returned to Times Square that evening. An intensely cold wind whistled through the neon lights and building-high displays. I enjoyed *Fiddler on the Roof* immensely but was overcome by family memories. At one time, Maris' aunt, a nun, took her holidays with us. Reverend Mother gave Auntie money to give to Maris for house keeping. Maris decided to bust the lot on a show. So the whole family, Maris, me, the four kids and Auntie saw *Fiddler on the Roof*. Outside after, the weather was freezing, down to minus five degrees. It was made all the more uncomfortable by my failing to find the subway entrance. After such an emotional evening I needed a beer. But the cans I had snuck into my room back at the hostel had frozen solid.

The next day I visited the Empire State Building, after standing in long queues where the patient tourists were harassed by raucous touts flogging tickets for just about every attraction in New York. They even took our photos and tried to sell them. Next I found the United Nations Building where I joined a tour and inspected the General Assembly and the

Security Council. That evening I visited the Metropolitan Opera at the Lincoln Centre and saw *The Barber of Seville*. The snooty couple next to me weren't interested in talking. The subway trip back to the hostel was unusually quiet. Outside the streets were deserted. If there was ever a time to be accosted, this was it. Fortunately for me, it was so cold even the muggers had sought refuge.

The second half of my New York stay followed the same sort of pattern. A highlight of my morning walk to the subway was a newspaper vendor so wrapped up in clothing that I saw nothing but his eyes and surrounding black skin. Those eyes spoke of misery and a desperate hope that he could sell the last of his few newspapers and go home. I wished I had asked him for a photo; it would have won a competition.

One day I visited St Patrick's Cathedral and lit a candle for Maris. Out of nowhere a desperate feeling of loneliness overwhelmed me. I sat in a pew and wept. All the feelings of loss, grief, guilt and regret flooded back. I was having a major wallop, indeed. I had to talk to someone. What could I do? I couldn't bail up a stranger and expect a hearing. This was cold, indifferent New York. Perhaps one of the priests?

I saw a notice that Confessions were being heard that morning. I hadn't been to Confession for decades. It was a weekly practice in my youth but the habit had gone out of fashion. I waited in my pew. I saw a young priest emerge from behind the altar and enter a confessional. I liked the look of him so I joined his queue. Just as I reached its head, an older priest shuffled from the front and entered the other confessional but I didn't like the look of him and decided to wait for the other. The fellow behind me in the queue prodded me.

'He's ready,' he said in a voice I thought too loud for a church. I succumbed to his pressure and entered the box.

Memories of the harangues I received in my youth in the confessional for my transgressions (usually impure thoughts and 'self abuse') aroused my anxiety as I knelt in the darkened confines. Okay, I thought, let's get on with it. I skipped the usual formula and went straight into my story. I had just been widowed. My wife had taken her own life. We were sexually active. I missed sex and was tempted to masturbation. The priest turned out to be a kindly old bloke who said it was a passing phase and, as well as giving me absolution, wished me luck, a nice human touch, I thought. It was a relief to tell my story and receive his support. My confession had the desired therapeutic result.

I like to imagine Maris set this up. I was probably due for a major wallop, and, if ever there was a place to have one, a church with Confession on hand was the place. During my trip, I frequently had a sense of Maris' presence. I was finding my way around strange cities. Incidents occurred which could be described as coincidental but could also be viewed as an invisible guiding hand. In my self-talk I engaged in conversation telling her my experiences. The mystic belief in her continuing existence had to accommodate the rational. I knew that she wasn't here, she was back in the Frenchs Forest Bush Cemetery, that I was on my own and my feelings told me I missed her physical presence. Within me coexisted vastly different views of my world, an inner vision that was warm and lively, full of wonder and conversation with Maris, an outer view that could have been cold and isolated, indifferent to or bored with my surroundings. The inner vision sustained me, opened my eyes and allowed me to be surprised by my new experiences.

My beliefs are by no means invincible. They're full of doubts and contradictions.

My last night in New York I attended the concert at Carnegie Hall. The conductor was Andre Previn who looked older and walked with a stoop. The orchestra — Oslo Philharmonic — played Ravel and Gershwin. I was seated in a box on the third tier with one other person, a charming African American lady, who knew the New York cultural scene.

'What's it really like living in New York,' I asked.

'Any place where you work and have your friends is home.'

The next day I took the train to JFK airport. The flight to London was uneventful and the lady sitting next to me remained uncommunicative, disinclined to talk to a lonely old Australian, keen to share his vision of the world. How I wished Maris was sharing the flight. I took the opportunity to read Brenda's *The Power of Now* just in case...

CHAPTER 13

Dear Noel,
As I write I am listening to a beautiful quiet song by
Shostakovich, and I am reminded once again of the
'eternal' that I believe surpasses our individual person-
alities. We are much more then we appear, so I believe
Maris' spirit is eternal as ours is.

I heard about the tragic incident on the morning of the
funeral. It was too late for me to re-arrange. But I have
thought of Maris a lot in the intervening days. I thought
of the wonderful time we had at the Albert Hall and her
good company in London. I have thought of her concern
and care, her work as a nurse, and generally her lovely
presence. I knew nothing of the pain she was experiencing,
It's all a mystery, our journey here, and it doesn't become
any less mysterious — as I've discovered.
Brenda

I had fond memories of our earlier visit to London.
In 1997 I attended a conference in Dublin and
Maris joined the partners' programme. On the way
home we stayed with Brenda.

When I arrived in the UK Brenda was very welcoming.

She was on her own. Graeme, her husband, was still in Sydney and due to arrive in a few days. We walked along the Thames near their home, rugged up against the cold wind blowing across the water, and had a great chat about St Anthony's in its earlier days. We discussed *The Power of Now*. I was pleased I had read it. In the evening we went to the Coliseum Theatre to see *On the Town*, an enjoyable musical performed by the English National Opera. Brenda devoted the whole of the next day to me. We took the bus into London central, came by Westminster Abbey and got off at Westminster Bridge, walked along South Embankment to the Globe Theatre where we joined a tour. Back at Niton Street we found ourselves locked out. Brenda sought the help of a neighbour. While we waited for the locksmith, we walked down the road to the local pub and had tea of sausages and mash. The problem was a key in the lock and after a hefty call-out fee for Sunday evening we found ourselves inside. We spent the rest of the evening chatting, sharing our visions of the world.

Brenda was busy so I spent the next day on my own. I visited the British Museum because I was keen to see the Elgin Marbles. Maris and I had visited the Parthenon from where they had been 'stolen'. We were told the Greek Government wanted them back, but the British Museum had other ideas. I was keen to see St Paul's. Last time we flashed by in a whirlwind tour. St Paul's was inspiring. Despite the crowds it maintained a prayerful atmosphere. I lit another candle for Maris. There was a small card with the candle. It read:

Jesus said
I am the light of the world
No follower of mine shall walk in darkness
A candle is a reminder
It recalls Jesus, the one true light,
whom the darkness could not extinguish.
A candle is a parable
burning itself out, it gives light to others.
A candle is a symbol
it speaks of light, hope, warmth and love.
A candle is a sign
It reminds us of the prayers of God's people

While I did not have the same intense emotional reaction as in St Patrick's in New York, I was sad and sat with my grief. I would have been happy to die there and then and join Maris, except that it would have been messy for the family to get my body back to Australia.

That small card gave me hope and from that day I became attached to candles. Their light dispels the darkness. I light one in memory of Maris whenever I visited a new church. I've bought them as gifts and to keep Maris' candle company. That day at St Paul's I bought one for Brenda.

I was looking forward to my first visit to France. I've been interested in the language since I studied French at school and always wanted to use my French in a French speaking country. I would have visited France years before but Maris had a fear of 'something happening' to me in a non-English speaking country and finding herself stranded. I felt guilty at the thought that her death had released me and made the trip possible.

At Charles de Gaulle airport I was determined to use public transport even if it meant going up the occasional blind alley. The first alley was the purchase of an Air France bus ticket to Orsay, which would have been a very long way around but I managed to get a refund and caught the shuttle bus and the metro to Maubert Mutualité, a short walk to my studio apartment at rue des Carmes. A welcoming bottle of red wine was on the table.

Then followed eight days of sightseeing. I was living in the Latin Quarter in the middle of the Sorbonne so many famous buildings were nearby. The Pantheon was up the road and next to it I found St Etienne du Mont where I lit a candle. I walked to the Luxembourg Gardens, back to the Seine with its bouquinistes (book sellers) and to Notre Dame. At both churches there was a book in which one could write down a prayer or a request. In my best French I wrote a prayer for Maris and a request that I would get through okay.

I wished Maris was with me to share the beauty of this marvelous city. A constant sorrow and sense of loss accompanied my wonder. I spent a day at the Louvre. One could spend days there. That evening I found an internet café used by the Sorbonne students. I checked some of the French language courses available. Courses were available at Chambéry or Annecy in the south east. I considered possibilities.

The next day I took the metro early to the Tour Eiffel. Saturday was my day to visit the Arc de Triomphe. I walked the full length of the Champs Elysées, which is easy, downhill all the way. The footpath is wide and I would imagine once upon a time it was a fashionable boulevard for promenading. Maris would have loved the stroll. I was disappointed to see a McDonald's and a stack of discount stores, a sacrilege on such a famous avenue. They robbed the avenue of its romance. I was not seeing what I wanted to see, but a scene given over to the tourists, closer to the reality of today's Paris. I wanted to be a traveller, not just a tourist, experiencing a new land, treading well worn paths, conscious that millions had gawked at these beautiful buildings before me and would continue after my visit.

On Palm Sunday I attended Mass at St Etienne's. Because I had been to Mass each day since I arrived in Paris, I had really grown to love that church. I felt less like a tourist as I joined in the prayers. We had the full works with several priests, an army of altar boys, incense, organ and full choir. I was able to follow every word using my Prions en Eglise (Let us pray in Church) which I had bought the night before. The gospel was the Passion according to St Mark, read by three readers. They had chosen their best readers for this special feast day. Their articulation was excellent, making it easy for me to listen and to follow. Even though Maris would not have understood a word, I'm sure she would have enjoyed the spectacle.

The following day I set out early by train for Versailles. I walked from the station to the chateau but found it shut. It's closed on Mondays. A film crew with all its paraphernalia had taken up the front court yard. I walked around to the back to the gardens but found it in winter mode with gardens bare, statues covered, pools and fountains empty. In the afternoon I visited the Jardin du Luxembourg and watched the old men playing chess. I had seen lovers together all over Paris but this was the first time I noticed gay lovers on the park benches — young men in business suits as if they had whipped out of the office for an afternoon's affection.

The evening Mass was special. The gospel reading was the story of Veronica washing the feet of Jesus and wiping them with her hair. Judas complains about the cost of the ointments. The young priest based his homily on this reading. He described Judas as offering despair but in Veronica's there was hope. I was pleased I had sufficient French to obtain a message, very similar to the messages from the Passionists at St Anthony's. Hope was a constant theme of their homilies.

On my last day in Paris I took the train to Charles de Gaulle airport. I was puzzled when told I had to change at Gare du Nord. Everyone got off and after reading the signs and listening to the announcements I managed to find my way up and down stairs and escalators to the right platform. There was an air of chaos and confusion, people walking in all direction in search of a connection. On the train I overheard an anxious man in a business suit on his mobile apologizing for being late for his appointment. There had been a strike, he explained. I was pleased I had enough French to eavesdrop and understand the drift of a conversation.

My nine day visit to Paris was just a taste. I now understand the way people rave about Paris — a beautiful city with the capacity to enchant. It's a city of lovers. I noticed so many couples pressing their young slender bodies together in passionate kisses, and I, an elderly foreigner watching, wishing I had my Maris with me, so that the magic could infect us both, too, and ignite the desires of our youth.

One day I would return. On the flight home I thought about my seven weeks of travel. I was in transition, learning to be a single, rather than one of a couple. On the surface, I had completed an around the world trip, but in my inner world, I was forced to admit, I hadn't gone far at all.

CHAPTER 14

Dear Noel and family,
At the time of Maris' untimely death I felt so shocked
and thus have left it sometime before writing. Maris
was such a beautiful and special person and as cousins
growing up we looked up to her with such a special
warmth. We loved visiting the family at Katamatite and
always a wonderful day was spent with such hospitality.
After our father Joe's early death it was Uncle Don and
Auntie Ellie who reached out to us with such kindness.
Maris had the same love and caring attitude as them.

You will have no doubt millions of these memories
of your own, and it is by remembering and sharing that
you will continue on with your lives.

Mary

I slept Good Friday evening at Angela's after catching up on the family news. In the morning I could not find my cross and chain. I had a memory of hanging them on the chair in the apartment in Paris. Did I leave them there? Later that day I sent an email to the owner. I received a reply. No, the cleaners had found nothing.

Angela told me that my brother-in-law Joe had been in

hospital for two weeks with lung problems. A family email had mentioned that Joe was in hospital but no one had told me how serious his problem was. I was annoyed that I wasn't told. Maria didn't want to spoil my holiday, I was told. Joe was okay now, even though he was on oxygen at home. I did not trust them. I wanted to see for myself.

After a week back home I drove to Queensland. Joe was on the mend but by no means over his illness. His doctor had discussed the possibility of a lung operation later in the year. I spent three days catching up on their news and showing them photos.

I did the trip to Queensland in one day but decided to take an overnight break at Hallidays Point on the way back to Sydney. At one time we owned a weekender at Blackhead Beach, a beautiful spot which had avoided the developers for so long but they were now in the process of covering the surrounding hills with ugly suburban brick houses. We had many family holidays and memories. I loved the place. I looked forward to our breaks there and seemed to plan my life around them. In winter it was just as pleasant. We had installed a wood heater which made the house so snug and cosy. When Maris was well, she too enjoyed her breaks in our quaint little wooden house which we had so carefully refurbished. She read while I listened to my vinyls. We were close to the beautiful beaches and everything was in walking distance. It was possible to never need the car. We even thought we might retire there.

When she was not well, she worried about the place. If I died first, she might not be able to sell. In one particularly blue period, she persuaded me to approach the local estate agent who was only too willing to list our property. Houses

at Hallidays Point seemed on average to take two years to sell
and I hoped I had enough time to see a change in heart on
Maris' part as I most definitely did not want to sell. But an
offer came within two months and my counter offer, which I
thought would be refused, was accepted. With great sadness
we left. I grieved deeply. Every nerve of my body revolted
against signing the contract. I think Maris was concerned at
the depth of my grief. She bought me a local artist's paint-
ing of the beach which hangs in my home office. At first I
refused to revisit Halliday's Point. It would be too painful. But
now five years later, I had adjusted to the loss, I thought.

I arrived at Hallidays Point about 3 pm. I walked along the
familiar beaches. My favourite was a secluded beach which
required a little agility to reach. I thought of the many times
I scrambled down the rocks. I sat on the sand. The ocean was
dazzling that day just as it always was. I thought of the many
times I'd visited, of the sense of timelessness and communion with God and nature I experienced as the waves rolled
endlessly towards the sand. No sound but the water and the
seagulls. This beach was one of my sacred places, as good as
or better than any church for refreshing the spirits.

I visited our old house. No one was home. I looked into
the windows and could see our furniture left as part of the
deal. There was the couch and table which I had brought up
from Sydney in my trailer, the green enamel wood heater, the
carpet which Maris agonised over and turned out to be too
light, the rugs to cover it in the high traffic areas. Even the
crockery in the dresser was ours. The scene was so familiar
but it was foreign.

The store where I used to chat to the owner was around
the corner opposite the main beach. The proprietor was a

stranger. A number of locals were gathered outside. They were indifferent and ignored me. I even sensed hostility; just another nuisance day tripper. I felt an immense sadness as I thought of the happy times we had spent together, not just here but everywhere. Gone for ever! I had planned to stay overnight but I thought I might as well be sad back home as in a lonely motel room. I got into my car and drove straight to Sydney.

How would I cope, living on my own in my five bedroom house? I took stock of the huge task ahead. I could be easily overwhelmed. It could be too much. You hear stories of widowers not coping. Used to their wives doing all the practical tasks such as cooking, housework, shopping, social organising, they are lost once they have to fend for themselves. Fortunately, I had learned to cook. Maris used to work three evenings a week. On those evenings I cooked my dinner and did the ironing in front of the television. I often cooked her lunch before she went to work. I looked forward to the evenings she was home. We enjoyed a beer before dinner, discussed the day's events and drank a glass or two of wine with our meal. Now I had to dine alone with no company except for Vetbill. Whenever I was preparing a meal, she would come padding from where she had been sleeping across the family room to join me in the kitchen. Whenever I watched television Vetbill sat on my lap. I enjoyed her silent company but I could not discuss the day's events.

How I missed the little chats at the end of the day and all the routines that two people develop over forty years. How I missed her greeting as I came home, usually, 'How did you go?' As I walked around our home, up and down the stairs, I could feel Maris' presence everywhere. Her clothes hung in the wardrobe. The family photos she had gathered over the years hung on the walls and sat on top of the sideboard.

The pain of loss was just as intense. Instead of moving me on, my travelling had merely distracted me. My grief was waiting, lurking in the corridors and rooms and ready to pounce. I lay in our bed at night and thought of her constantly. Grief was the price I had to pay for our intimacy. The curves of her body were just as exciting to me as when we were first married. She was attractive rather than beautiful when we first met, but she matured into her beauty and elegance. I remember with pride and even a pang of jealousy some of my male acquaintances referring to her as 'the beautiful Mrs. Braun.'

How I missed our love making. I had fantasies of her running her soft hands over every part of my body and me in turn moving my hands over and around her. I experienced a strong need but had no means of expressing it. It was my Maris that I desired and no one else. Her body, her lips, her kisses. I felt myself caressing my own breasts, stomach and my hands descending further, imagining they were Maris'. I had a terrible duality between the body and the spirit. This is what every widower must face, I thought — a tug of war between the spirit and the flesh. I wondered around the house naked, looked at my body in the mirror and said to myself, 'I'm a fit man, with all the healthy appetites that God has given mankind, but I've lost the means of expressing them.'

One night stands did not appeal, nor did becoming a habitué of prostitutes. The battle between my Catholic upbringing and my sensual nature was under way. Matters which hadn't been of consequence since my youth confronted me. I was thrown back into my pre-marriage days when my Church frowned severely on masturbation and sex out of marriage. Both were grievous sins. I remembered being relieved that marriage removed me from my torments.

Today, forty years later, we live in a new world. Social change has made non-marital sex widely acceptable, and the decline of religious belief has released sex from moorings that were immensely powerful and loaded with sin. Health authorities regard masturbation as a harmless activity and normal for a person in my circumstances. These days even the Church seemed to have softened its stand. That did not remove or lessen my deeply ingrained guilt, a legacy of my youth. I did not thank Maris for my enforced celibacy, for throwing me floundering into this confusion, this conflict. People joke about Catholic guilt but it is real to the sufferer.

Added to my agony was the guilt that continued to engulf me over my failure to protect Maris from herself. I could not dispel from my mind that I'd failed her. Her pain had exceeded her resources for coping. I tried to help her to find a way. It wasn't enough. I prayed that I had the resources to cope with my own vulnerability, to resist the temptations to lapse into despair as I struggled to make sense of what had happened and to give meaning back into my life.

Morning was the worst time. I would wake early, dreading the arrival of the new day, my stomach already in a knot. The demons that rose to the surface in the night continued to threaten me with a dawn of silent despair. In those precarious hours, I argued with myself. I should be able to decide what this day should be like. I should make a choice of what to set down on the blank page handed to me each morning, to refuse to settle for what at first sight seems inevitable, namely, a sequel to yesterday's sad and guilty thoughts. As I showered, shaved and cleaned my teeth, I struggled with my cloud of fears, hoping for a healing shaft of light to disperse the demons. I prayed. I repeated my formula of C's and S's.

Each day began with this painful, prayerful approach. Everything was disjointed. Sometimes I had to stop and start again until I got the rhythm right. I refused to allow myself to limply succumb to the negative charges. I was like one of the spiders outside in my garden, every day repairing webs as they twinkled with sunlight in the morning dew.

Usually the heavy dark lifted, the demons retreated snarling and I was able to breathe more freely. In the daytime I settled back with a fierce mental and physical energy into the routines. I needed structure, a programme of activities to keep me busy. I walked to the cemetery two or three times a week. I had my chats with Maris. I took Lifeline shifts, including overnights. Kathie the counselling manager asked me if I was ready to see individual face-to-face clients. I said I was. Workloads from the Australian Bureau of Statistics were waiting and becoming drearier by the day. I enrolled at the local gym for a twelve month program. I was keen to keep fit. I did not want my grief to turn me into a slob. I went to Catenian meetings, grateful for the support the brothers had given me. I attended church. I edited the Terrey Graph. I received and accepted invitations to dinner. A widowed lady from church advised me to accept them while they lasted. I had my own network and I had now inherited Maris'.

I was determined my home would not turn into a bachelor's camp. I bought flowers, arranged a shrine for Maris and kept the place tidy. Each morning I made my bed carefully. I shaved and showered daily. I mowed the lawn and weeded the garden. The wallaby grass was doing well. Maris' tree had put on a few more centimetres. I had a problem with gardening because that was Maris' interest. To see her working in the garden was a sign she was feeling better. When I worked in the garden my thoughts turned to her and the sadness of loss returned. Sometimes I had to stop and retreat inside.

I was vulnerable. One day I visited Manly and, conscious of my unfulfilled needs, drifted into its sex shop, not before furtively looking along the walkway. What a curious array of merchandise! I cast my eyes over the DVDs. Their covers described in lurid terms their contents. There was a wide range to choose from. I selected a DVD made in Queensland featuring three couples. The contents were ultra erotic and the plot was hopeless but I grew attached to those couples and remembered their names. They were enthusiastic and enjoyed each other's company, intent on giving mutual pleasure. Their range of love making activities was far more extensive than what Maris and I ever imagined, but I recognised some of our own repertoire. I had the guilts about this item of pornography in my house and I threw it out with the rubbish but I missed my Queensland couples and a week later, I'm forced to admit, I revisited the sex shop and bought another copy.

Angela rang or visited me every few days. She missed her mother desperately. She said she had to keep an eye on me as I was the only parent she had. One day I said to her, 'Don't be surprised if you find the odd Penthouse lying about.'

'That's okay, Dad.' She laughed. 'I'll just put them away and lend you some of Guy's.'

How I loved Angela for her support. We frequently hugged each other and shed our tears together.

* * *

The first game of the AFL season is always full of hope and anticipation. Perhaps this will be the year that Swans win the flag despite the fact that some of the Melbourne pundits had predicted that Sydney would take the wooden spoon.

How would I cope with the season? Maris and I attended all the games. How we enjoyed them. In fact, Maris was the more enthusiastic. She had been brought up in a football loving family. We loved to post mortem the Swans' game and dissected each player's contribution, read the analysis of results in the Sydney Morning Herald and the paper's predictions for next week's round.

Angela offered to come with me to the first match. I was so grateful. That game was more than just a football game. Good news, the Swans defeated Hawthorn by 63 points.

As we made our way home after the match, Angela told me she had more good news.

'Dad, the children were playing in the room you slept in. Hugh crawled under the bed and came up with Mum's cross and chain.'

How I was relieved! I was resigned to never seeing that cross again. It was almost as if a little piece of my life, a link with Maris, had been restored.

CHAPTER 15

Passionist Missionaries, Boroko, Papua New Guinea
Dear Noel,
As I'm writing this I recall the sense of shock and sadness I experienced when Pam Clark let me know of Maris' death; it was difficult to take it in completely at the time. And now I have a sense of shame that I have taken so long to contact you personally. But I want to write to you now. You and Maris and the family have been, and are, very good friends to me, and though my silence may have indicated that I have forgotten you, that certainly isn't so.

Your own comment in the December Terrey Graph struck me, as it revived so many memories in me. Maris truly was a person who brought a calmness and a peace to others, as I have experienced. And only recently I heard one of my Passionist brothers talk about the depression he experiences in his life; it is an 'insidious affliction'.

But what I really want to say is that my heart goes out to you, and all the family, Angela and Guy, Jacinta, Stephen and Tim, and their partners who are part of the family now. I can't imagine what Maris' death has done to you, but simply want to be with you. Your

faith-inspired comment about believing that 'Maris is now on another journey' stirs up my own faith. In your 'thank you' for what others have given to you, you are still giving to others.
    Peace,
    Tony

I continued to attend church but it wasn't the same. During my absence St Anthony's had undergone significant change. The parish had begun in the early seventies under the pastorship of the Passionists. Father Peter was our first pastor, and he was followed by Fathers Tony, Tom, Michael and Brendan. Father Peter had commenced the Family Group Movement as a means of community building. A dozen or so families met regularly, supported each other, grieved with each other and celebrated with each other. St Anthony developed an outstanding sense of community and welcome. Not only were the Passionists good priests but fine human beings as well, men of compassion and conviction who preached the gospel of love from the heart. Their homilies were great. They preached a message that had meaning to our everyday lives. I left the church uplifted. Going to church had been a joyful experience, a highlight of the week.

There had been a growing anxiety that the Passionists were running out of men. They were getting older, numbers were leaving the Order and there were no younger men in training. Their decline was a reflection of the general decline in numbers among priests. Our Father Brendan was the youngest and could become the last to turn out the lights. Sooner or later, they would have to withdraw from some of the Australian parishes they served. We hoped and prayed that St Anthony's would not be one of them. All these happenings were like a glowing gloom before an approaching storm front. Gradually, the storm clouds gathered over St. Anthony's, high, dark, menacing and thorough, until a great wall of rain and heavy wind drenched the parish in confusion. In the middle of 2004, the leadership of the Passionists announced their withdrawal from a number of parishes, including St Anthony's. The news astonished the parishioners. Anxious times were ahead and in the absence of detail about the parish's future, people's imagination filled the gap. People felt betrayed and suspicious. The Passionists had walked out on them, the diocese would close the parish and sell the land, they believed, despite the Bishop's reassurances.

The formal handing back of the parish to the Bishop took place at a ceremony while I was away. It was a time, I was told, of great sadness, many tears and a great sense of loss.

When I returned from my travels I found a new priest, Father Barry, who had spent the last 38 years in New Guinea, facing a huge personal challenge of reintegrating into the Australian culture and running a parish in deep shock. The sense of loss was profound. The conspiracy theorists among the parishioners worked overtime. Father Barry had been set up to fail, the people would drift away, and the Bishop would be 'forced' to close because the numbers were so small.

I felt a double sense of loss. Not only had I lost my wife, but I had lost my Passionists as well, both core to my existence. After attending my first Mass under the new order, I said to one of my fellow parishioners, 'We're back in the Catholic Church.'

I am not sure why I continued to attend St Anthony's. Why
did I bother? Why did I not drift away like so many others?
Perhaps it was a sense of loyalty, much the same loyalty that
made me stick with the Sydney Swans in their dark days
when they looked as if they'd never win a game. I was no fair
weather supporter of the Swans and I had the same loyalty
to St Anthony's, I suppose. I asked myself what Maris would
have done. I heard her saying, 'Stick with it, Noel. Give it
a go. The consistent messages of our Passionists was hope.
Things will improve.'

Perhaps it was my fellow parishioners, the people who
knew us as Maris and Noel, as a couple, who supported me.
Now I was Noel, just one. I had a new identity. Another
widower from the church had complained that after his wife
died he did not feel welcome, but I never experienced that.
I was lonely coming to church on my own but after church
it was different. People talked to me, wanted to know how I
was coping and about my trip. Although I may have found
the liturgy uninspiring, I felt uplifted once I was outside and
talking. The Passionists had left, but their spirit of welcome
remained. The community spirit was strong and people were
compassionate. Other churches seemed to be full of individual worshippers more concerned with saving their own
souls than with talking to others. I was interested to hear
from some who, in their disappointment, shopped around
for another church but had returned to St Anthony's with the
comment, 'It's worse out there.'

I was also a member of the universal church. I had been
brought up a Catholic and had attended a Catholic school.
Maris too had received a Catholic education and her faith
had been nurtured by her family. Our faith bound us together.

Like any human institution the Catholic Church has its faults and criticism is easy. However, I valued its traditions and was happy to let the world know I was a Catholic. The church professes a set of ideals but it also recognises its members are sinners who often fail to measure up. Although its leaders are human and can be judgmental and condemning, it also professes the forgiveness of sinners. One can make a fresh start. Few faiths carry such compassionately repeated opportunities for repair, recovery and renewal. The church offers hope and love. It gives the strength to keep on going.

My faith and belief in God needed nurturing. It had received a severe buffeting and although I had not rejected God for taking Maris from me, I was fragile. I was reeling in self-doubt, guilt and grief. I felt a sinner who had made many, many mistakes. I needed to remain. To quit going to church would be resorting to despair.

* * *

The weather was still hot in May. I was pleased because I had spent two months in the cold of the Northern Hemisphere winter. I decided to go for a swim. But this time I chose the nudist beaches in the Sydney Harbour National Park, isolated little beaches out of the public gaze that take a little agility to access.

As I scrambled down the washed out path, I thought of the words of Kate, my counsellor. She said the suicide of a loved one changes people. They do things they have never done before. This was the first time I had visited an official nudist beach. I thanked God for the beauty of this little beach and for the sense of freedom to my soul, my spirit, my mind and my body my nakedness gave me. I had stepped out of my comfort zone. I could not offend with my nudity because everyone else was nude. Skinny-dipping was liberating. To feel the water rushing by my thighs! I thought how nice it would be to skinny dip with Maris, but that was pure fantasy because she couldn't swim. We had been naked together many times in the privacy of our bedroom, but never in a public place. It was a delicious thought, however, to imagine us lying together in the warm sun.

I could hear her warning me to be careful so I smothered myself with sun cream. My skin was white, in contrast to the tanned bodies around me, mostly male. I found myself admiring those bodies, made in the image of God although many were quite imperfect specimens. What a piece of work is man! My admiration of the male form made me wonder about changes in my own identity. Many of the men attracted to the beach were probably gay. Was I leaning that way, too, after so many years of heterosexuality? Just another fear, just another torment.

Before the beginning of June, the weather turned cold and that was the end of my sunbathing.

CHAPTER 16

Dear Noel,
On occasions like this there are no words to adequately
convey the shock and sorrow I felt as I was not aware
Maris had such an affliction and no idea she had borne
it for so long. When I consider it, I think we only caught
up on two occasions over the last twenty years, where
we both remarked that Maris looked exactly the same
as she did forty years ago, with not the slightest hint
of what she was enduring. A valiant effort under the
circumstances.

It must be consoling to have kept up with your faith
over the years; I could not see how anyone would cope
under these circumstances if they had no faith at all. I
wish you every success in re-constructing your life, Noel.
I hope with God's help you have the strength to move.
Peter

I am very thankful I had *Friend and Philosopher.* If I
had only half written the book at the time of Maris'
death, I doubt whether I would have had the commitment, motivation and conviction to continue. But I had
done the hard work, written many drafts and brought it up to

publishing standard. It was ready to be released on the public. In my dark night of confusion I needed a purpose, a reason to continue because sometimes, particularly in the middle of the night, I couldn't see much point without Maris.

Promoting *Friend and Philosopher* gave me purpose.

I was looking forward to getting my hands on it. The publisher emailed that *Friend and Philosopher* had arrived in Australia and was waiting at a warehouse in Tullamarine. We had arranged initially to print 1000 copies. I would take 700 and the other 300 would go to the book distributor to supply retailers.

I had already decided to spend two weeks in Melbourne and drove down late May. I needed to be with family, to maintain the strong bonds forged in the fire of Maris' death. Bereavement in some families drives them apart, but I was hopeful that our closeness would be enhanced. I shared my time with Tim and Melissa, and with my brother Tom and his wife Robyn. My visit coincided with two Swans games. I saw both with Tim. I was dismayed to witness my team being badly beaten by St Kilda. Everything that could go wrong went wrong. It was all doom and gloom. However, the Swans stuck at it, bounced back the next week and thrashed Carlton. On both occasions, the coach was philosophical, keeping things in perspective. A good lesson on dealing with life?

Having lived in Melbourne for forty-five years, I had friends to contact. My trip down became a pilgrimage into the past, into the life that Maris and I shared before my employer of the time moved me to Sydney. I wanted to renew old friendships. I was particularly heartened to catch up with my old mates, Barry and John. We courted our wives at the same time. Barry and I were each others' best men. John married Bernice a week after our wedding. The three couples, Barry and Carol, John and Bernice, Maris and I, had come together to celebrate our fortieth wedding anniversaries in March 2003. We spent the weekend at Barry and Carol's beach house in Sorrento. What fun we had over a few drinks reminiscing and talking about our families. We were witness to three happy and successful marriages; married until death do us part. We enjoyed ourselves so much we thought we should get together again. It was not to be.

I enjoyed seeing Peter and Barbara, friends from our early years of marriage. They were keen to know details of Maris' depression and the lead up to her death. I was comfortable enough to tell them. In fact, I found it beneficial to repeat the story to these friends of a previous era.

I took a trip to Airey's Inlet, a small village on the south coast of Victoria beyond Geelong. When we lived in Melbourne, we built a weekender near the Fairhaven Life Saving Club. I had many fond memories of the three golden summers we spent there. Maris would move in with our young family for the whole summer. I joined them for the Christmas and New Year holidays. I had not visited Airey's Inlet for over twenty years and as I drove down I imagined that by now the developers would have found this idyllic place, cleared the surrounding hills and covered them with an imitation of suburbia. But I was surprised to find Airey's much the same. The surrounding hills were still green and most of the buildings were hidden in trees. I went looking for the site of our house. A fire storm had destroyed it along with the rest of Airey's Inlet in the Ash Wednesday bushfires of 1983. By that time we had moved to Sydney and sold our house. A much bigger dwelling had replaced our humble fibro and timber abode. Money had found Fairhaven. Being a weekday in June, there was no one about. I walked around the streets noting that all the houses had been rebuilt, much bigger and grander in style. I could not remember if the surf club was the same building. I gazed on the beach just below and so many memories flooded back. Maris sitting under a broad hat and umbrella protecting her fair skin from the harsh summer sun. Tim in his pram. Memories of shark alarms, of the children dashing in and out of the water, of their involvement in Little Nippers, of the regular visits to the pub for an evening drink after a day on the sand.

I remember one evening the life savers laughing about a 'ruthless' girl playing British Bulldog who bowled over all the boys and made some cry. I joined in the laughter, then realised they were talking about my Angela. How I enjoyed relating that story to Maris. She was mortified. The surf club was the centre of a tight little community. I looked at the noticeboard and the rosters and recognised some family names from our days. A new generation had taken over. As I leant on the rail overlooking the beach, a sad breeze blew over the grey winter sea and I felt nostalgia as sharp as the wind.

Back in Geelong I stayed overnight with Maris' cousin, Kevin and his wife Margie. Kevin was a medical practitioner. He had been working for many years at Taree and we saw him regularly during our visits to Hallidays Point. Kevin moved to Geelong for better opportunities for the children. Kevin asked about Maris' depression and the treatment she had been receiving. He was also interested in how I, the survivor, was faring. He described my behaviour as masochistic when I told him I had returned to Lifeline. He thought I should move away from anything to do with depression and suicide. His attitude made me think about my motivation and I found myself justifying my decision. I thought that by reaching out to help others, I was helping myself. I'm not sure if Kevin understood.

On the way back to Sydney, I detoured to Shepparton in the Goulburn Valley. Maris grew up in Katamatite, north of Shepparton. I was a regular visitor to the region in my courting days. I met the locals of Katamatite at church and in the pub and grew to love the Goulburn Valley. I regarded it as a kind of spiritual home because Maris had so many links. Her family had been farmers for generations; her father was a Stock and Station Agent, and well known for his expertise in judging sheep. We were married at St. Brendan's, the Catholic church of Shepparton, and many of Maris' relatives live in the surrounding district.

I stayed two nights with Norma and Doug, at Dookie, out of Shepparton. Norma and Maris did their nursing training together and had remained friends all their lives. They rang each other regularly, and went to nurses' reunions together while the kids and I stayed with Doug. During our time in Sydney we stayed with them overnight on our trips to Melbourne. I always enjoyed our visits and the kids loved to roam around Doug's farm, watch the sheepdogs herding the sheep, and play on Doug's tractors. The land was flat, dry and dusty, but nevertheless beautiful, particularly at dusk as the noises of the day retired into the silence of the night.

Norma and Doug were keen for me to maintain the friendship. Like so many others, they were not aware of the extent of Maris' depression. Norma gave me a photograph of them together, taken a month or so before I met her. That photo of two young, unsophisticated country lasses laughing in the snow of Mount Donna Buang moved me in unexpected ways. My mind raced back to the Heidelberg Town Hall where I saw this attractive, tall, slim, dark haired girl knocking back the fellows asking for a dance. My decision to try my luck had a profound influence on the direction of my life, on my destiny, probably the most profound and far-reaching of all the choices I have ever made

CHAPTER 17

Dear Noel
I find it hard to express my love and admiration for
Maris as a friend and nurse. She was a very special
person who enriched the lives of those who knew her
but you don't need me to tell you. Her kindness and
goodness and steady faith will remain.
Heather

Back in Sydney, no sooner had I unpacked my bag than I threw myself with frenzy into the promotion of *Friend and Philosopher*. My first market was the people who knew Maris and me. Even if they were not readers, they would buy in recognition of Maris and in support of me. Angela called it the sympathy vote. I approached our local book shop, the Good Book, at Belrose to place copies. The owner was supportive. He knew Maris, she was a regular customer. I approached other local bookshops, some accepting, and others indifferent. I contacted the *Manly Daily* suggesting I had a good story for an article. The editor agreed. I was thrilled that many local people read the article.

I reckoned Swan Hill would be a good area to canvass as

Friend and Philosopher is set in that area. I wrote to the Swan Hill Library and they ordered five copies. I was delighted. My success made me think of other libraries. I wrote to all the public libraries in Australia.

I wrote to all the Catenian Circles in Sydney and Canberra offering my services as a guest speaker. I approached the local Rotary clubs. I had a few bites. In my talk I emphasised depression and its effect on the sufferers and their families. I indicated my book had been dedicated to Maris and that my profits would go to Lifeline.

Norma telephoned. 'The Shepparton News has printed a review. They reckon that *Friend and Philosopher* is very relevant to regional Australia because of its story of rural decline,' she said.

'Really?' It was great news.

'It sounds like regional Australia would be a good market,' she went on. 'Many communities have lost their battle to keep their schools open.'

Norma's news made me decide on a 'grand tour' or two of South East Australia. I would fit these tours into my other activities.

A prefect opportunity arose when the Sydney Swans won a place in the AFL Grand Final.

I rang Tim. 'If I got tickets to the Grand Final,' I said, 'would you come too?'

'Absolutely,' he said.

And so I camped out, arriving at the Sydney Cricket Ground in my Swans gear about 3.30 am. People were already lined up. I was thirty-ninth in the queue. Three ladies and a schoolboy arrived at the same time. The camaraderie was contagious and by the time we bought our tickets we were the best of friends. In the intervening hours we discussed every game, the various crucial incidents, the personal lives of the players, their form, sharing our mutual anxiety whether there were enough tickets left as there were only a few hundred available. The TV cameras were there. Sydney Swans had not won a premiership for seventy-five years. My four friends and I danced and hugged each other when we received our tickets. The TV people rushed over and made us repeat our joy. I saw myself on Channel Ten news that evening waving my tickets, yelling, 'Go Swannies!' A brief moment of notoriety.

Pity I wasn't waving my book! Instead, on the drive to Melbourne, I called at all the bookshops along the way.

What a game! Tim and I arrived at the Melbourne Cricket Ground at 10 am. We stood until 6 pm, not game to leave our spots. I saw and greeted all my friends from the queue. The tension was excruciating. The lead changed. Both sides made mistakes. The Swans were four points ahead. Seconds to go. Leaping Leo Barry made his famous match saving leap to grab the ball at the mouth of the West Coast Eagles goal. I found myself caught completely in the tension, imploring Maris to intervene. I'd like to think she said okay and guided that ball into Leo Barry's hands. Tim and I hugged each other, overcome by the euphoria. We shed a tear together for Maris who was not there to see the amazing win.

I drove home via Gippsland and the South coast, calling at bookshops along the way.

* * *

Stephen got a job in Tamworth so I drove up to visit him and Anthea. On the way up and down I visited the bookshops. A wise old bookseller at Armidale said, 'You will have to promote wherever you leave books, otherwise they will remain sitting on the shelf.'

So, I knocked on the doors of the newspapers at Armidale and Tamworth. I obtained my first ABC interview at Tamworth and also with the local commercial radio. This established the pattern of contacting the local newspaper and the radio stations wherever I went. I was surprised at myself, knocking on the doors of radio stations and asking to be interviewed. I could not imagine myself doing such a thing twelve months previously for fear of rejection. I had developed an indifference, an immunity to people's opinions. I wasn't outrageous but I think I was operating under a mantle of grief. Having experienced so much pain, getting an occasional knock back was nothing. Maris would have told me I was being cheeky.

I also felt a change in the way I wanted to express my faith. After decades of being settled in a mode of expression, I had become restless. I was a spiritual vagabond. Was there a better way of reaching God? I was confused. I could feel myself being distanced from the church even though I continued to attend. I just didn't feel spiritually enhanced. I was in the process of redefining myself. I was trying to survive, to rise above the disaster, to carry on with life after Maris. We went to church together and now I went alone. I could never expect things to be the same. I found I was being sustained more by talking quietly to God and to Maris directly, as if I was bypassing religious service and going straight to the Holy Spirit. I was getting more out of my quiet chats by

Maris' grave. Sometimes I wasn't sure whether I was talking to Maris or to God. I got them mixed up. I suppose it didn't matter. I visited Maris' grave at least twice a week, more often if a problem was worrying me. I'd sit on the bench near her grave, the sounds of the bush behind me and talk to her. Sometimes a course of action would spring to mind and I'd like to think that Maris planted the idea.

I found the Lifeforce Memorial Service helpful. Lifeforce is a suicide prevention program, organised by the Wesley Mission. It offers the memorial service so that those who have been touched by suicide have a place to come together in a spirit of comfort and hope. The service was held on the Northern Broadwalk behind the Opera House, the bleak winter wind blowing off the water. I felt I was with others who understood something of my journey. It was a comfort to know I was not alone. Others were prepared to sit with me in the rubble. The ceremony was peaceful and serene. We were invited to cast a sunflower into the Harbour as a gesture of love and remembrance. The sunflower is a symbol of life, brightness and hope. Its centre holds up to 2000 seeds and when it dies there is potential for new life. The service was non-religious, but I felt the presence of God reaching out to those in pain.

Sunday 30 October was the first anniversary of Maris' death. I wanted to do something special. I wanted to take over one of the St Anthony's Sunday Masses as a Memorial Mass and I wanted Father Peter to celebrate. He was very happy to be involved. Conscious of the church politics, I approached the Parish. I half expected to meet resistance as it was not the practice to ask for a Memorial Mass on a Sunday. Everyone was cooperative. I could have the Sunday 6 pm Mass.

I let everyone know, even inserted a notice in the Manly Daily. I invited my Lifeline fiends and all Maris' networks as well as my own. The church was full. Chris Lee the undertaker attended. Father Peter went to a lot of trouble. The Mass was a happy event, a celebration of Maris' life, a delightful mixture of the sacred and the profane. I placed her Sydney Swans scarf and cap on the altar and at the conclusion the Family Group emerged holding red and white balloons and dancing to the Swans theme song *Cheers, cheers, the red and the white*. I joined in the dancing. I presented a cheque to our Lifeline director Rod, my profits so far from my sales of *Friend and Philosopher*. Maris' spirit lives on.

* * *

Sometime in October Kate rang me wanting to know if I would be prepared to talk about my experience of coping at the Support After Suicide Group? The Group offered the opportunity to meet others who had suffered a similar loss. I had attended two meetings along with Angela. They were harrowing, I have to admit. At each meeting there were survivors just recently bereaved and their emotional scars were very raw indeed. Others had been attending for years and came long distances, believing this group was the only place where they felt their situation was understood. Tired of well-intentioned friends saying they should be moving on, they welcomed the non-judgmental and accepting atmosphere.

I remember one meeting when we spoke about the importance of symbols. I told the group how I had created a little shrine with Maris' photo, the cross from her coffin and a series of candles. I always kept fresh flowers nearby. Another man talked about a small rockery garden he had created for his daughter. A couple spoke of a beach on the North Coast where they had scattered their son's ashes because it was his favourite beach for surfing.

Kate asked me to talk about my efforts to reach out as my way of coping. I spoke about Lifeline and of the compulsive way in which I was promoting *Friend and Philosopher*. Another lady who had lost a son spoke about her work with a volunteer force supporting the police in their youth work.

I had a face-to-face meeting with Kate early in December. I raised the idea of writing some day about my experience as a suicide survivor. By writing about my own bereavement, I might help others who are facing a similar tragedy.

'It might help you, too,' Kate added.

Occasionally I took a step backwards. Anne wrote to me. Her husband Keith died about eighteen years previously. In an earlier letter, Anne had told me how Maris had supported her at the time with visits and casseroles. Would I be interested in attending a Jazz Ball organised by the Sydney Jazz Club?

I brooded. I talked to Angela. She gave her usual advice, 'Go for it, dad.' She joked that I was going on a date.

Anne asked me if I was comfortable about going. I lied and said yes. But was I really ready? As I drove to her place to pick her up, dressed in my tuxedo and sporting a mask, I shed a tear. I was being disloyal to Maris, I felt, dead just over one year.

We had a very good evening. Anne was a Sydney Jazz club regular. Everyone was dressed up, the ladies mostly in 1920s style with feathers and boas. The band was the Café Society Orchestra led by Geoffrey Ogden Brown. I was in a

time warp. All the tunes were from the 1920s, from *Puttin'
on the Ritz* to *Varsity Drag*. The dance floor was always full,
the dancers mostly of mature age. My impression was that
there were a lot of fit septuagenarians and octogenarians who
were members of the Sydney Jazz Club.

As we drove home discussing the evening, I wondered
what I would do if Anne invited me in for coffee. However,
in less time than it takes to say 'no thanks', she sprung out of
the car and made no arrangements to meet again.

I was thankful we did not take it any further. I had done
my job of being a partner for the evening. However, I was
grateful to Anne for the evening, a new experience for me. I
had mentioned the outing to family and a few friends. They
inquired as to how it went. People were curious, I suspect,
to know if I was ready to 'move on'. They saw the evening as
a first venture to meet and mix with the ladies. I knew I was
not ready. I wasn't sure if I ever would.

I had morning tea with another Anne. I sat next to her
earlier in the year at a NSW Writers' Centre writing course.
We told each other a little of our stories. She had been caring
for a very sick husband for some time. She was very interested
in my writing and bought a copy of *Friend and Philosopher*.
She emailed some very favourable comments. I thanked her
in my reply. She later emailed to tell me her husband had
died. Perhaps we could meet to discuss our mutual interest
in writing. She also wanted me to look over some of her own
writing. Over our cup of coffee, she told me of her husband's
illness. I could see she needed to talk just as I needed to talk
about Maris. She became concerned. Here she was, having coffee with a man just weeks after her husband's death.
What would friends think if they happened to walk in? As it

happened, a couple from St Anthony's did come in. I introduced Anne as a friend. I sensed her anxiety. Her comments raised the question. What was a respectable time to be seen in such company? This issue must confront every widow and widower.

My last marketing effort for 2005 was as guest speaker at the December of the Pittwater Catenians, my own circle. It was a gala occasion, being a ladies' night and the Christmas party. I had avoided the ladies' nights so far as I was very conscious of being on my own without partner. This night was different. I had a job to do. I was well received and felt among friends. I must say once more I was very grateful for the support from my brother Catenians.

* * *

My time of solitude ended when Jacinta, Rick and Brody arrived back in Australia for Christmas. How pleased I was to see my daughter back home. I had spoken to her often. She missed the family and whereas I could mourn with Angela, she was on her own. Our calls would sometimes end in tears as she, like Angela, missed her mum.

I showed Jacinta Maris' tree. It had grown to about two meters.

'You should cut it down, Dad, before it gets too big.'

I couldn't. I was not ready.

It was the second Christmas without Maris. The pain of loss is supposed to ease with time but the family found this Christmas more difficult. I think we were in shock the first year, but now we had twelve months to accept that she was gone.

I made my last visit for the year to Maris. I was exhausted, and needed to rest on the nearby seat as I had walked in thirty-three degree heat and was covered in sweat. I could hear Maris saying, 'You're mad, Noel, to be out in this heat.'

I cast my mind back over the last fourteen months. What a journey it had been, a time of constant vulnerability. Many times I was ready to join Maris in the top bunk. I kind of wanted to be with her without particularly wanting to die. I can appreciate the expert's opinion that the bereaved by suicide are a high risk group. What did I have without her?

I reviewed what I did have. I had my life, my health and fitness. I had my faith. I had my writing and my many interests. I had devoted so much energy and thought to promoting *Friend and Philosopher*. What might have been the outcome if I didn't have this goal, if I didn't have *Friend and Philosopher* as a major point of focus? A focus of intent that was sometimes white hot. Although grieving can plunge a person into depression, it can also engender tremendous energy. In my case, I transferred all that passion into promoting *Friend and Philosopher*, and was ready to work without respite. My marketing was protracted, relentless, and unflagging in its intensity to bring off a few sales.

As a consequence, I had learned new skills and developed a confidence to assert myself, to be indifferent to rejection, to challenge myself and to venture beyond my comfort zone.

I had also learned of the power of community. *No man is an island*. If I had isolated myself and faced my tragedy as an individual without family, without friends, if in turn I had not supported my family and friends, would I have survived?

CHAPTER 18

Dear Noel,
Maris was a very beautiful and extraordinary woman.
She personified love and kindness; her warmth lifted the
spirits of a room. I'll never forget the love and generosity
that she showed me. Even though Maris has left us, she
still continues to impact people's lives. Her life journey
has left footprints in the sand, and can never be washed
away. I know you always miss her, but I pray that God
will comfort you. I thank God everyday that he shared
her with us. God created and moulded a wonderful
woman who glorified him through service and love. I
pray for your family during this time of mourning and
hope you receive comfort soon.
Love from Rachel

All this while, I had been working on another manuscript — *Whistler Street*. The first draft had been completed before Maris died. Like *Friend and Philosopher* I wrote the first words many years previously and put it aside to attend to my career and family. Like *Friend and Philosopher*, I had sent away the manuscript to manuscript assessment agencies for advice. You post the manuscript, wait two or three months and back comes a report on its strengths and faults. As a writer I am more interested in criticisms than praise because I want to produce the best possible work. It is not enough to get your family or friends to read your book. It is nice to hear their praise but you need to subject your writing to a blowtorch. These assessments are invaluable. Sometimes the comments are brutal. You have to put your ego to one side. *Whistler Street* was undergoing the same process — appraisal, rewriting, and further appraisal.

Maris read the many drafts of *Friend and Philosopher*. She drew on her experience as a country girl to make suggestions. They added an authenticity to my descriptions of a small country town. She had read some selected pieces of *Whistler Street*. She had me tone down the sex scenes. A few weeks before her death when the depression had taken hold and she was doing little apart from reading, she had run out of books and offered to read the full manuscript. After an hour she could not continue as she found the theme too dark.

Maris had left behind a series of exercise books in which she wrote down her many thoughts. I had not delved into these. I had not even gone through her clothes in any detail. I decided I could get started on these tasks. I looked through Maris' exercise books. I looked over her clothes. She had many elegant outfits. I gently stroked one of my favourites, a cocktail dress in a series of shades of blue that made her look cool and refreshed, even on the hottest of days. In my mind's eye, I saw her wearing the dress at a function, quietly chatting to the people and listening to their stories. I realised I still wasn't ready. Her clothes could wait.

Instead I renewed my promotion of *Friend and Philosopher*.

I wrote to all the secondary schools in the Eastern states. That idea arose from Fiona. Her 17 year old son had read *Friend and Philosopher*. He had enjoyed it and commented that it told a story of an Australia that he didn't know. That inspired me to think that the story would appeal to teenagers and every school should know of it.

I planned a number of 'grand tours' to fit in with other activities. My first trip was to the Gold Coast. I enjoyed staying with Maria and Joe. They live in a retirement village and Maria proudly introduced me to her friends as 'my brother, the author' as if I was famous, not a beginning writer doing his best to flog his first book. The industry uses terms such as 'emerging', 'developing' or 'aspiring' writers. I think I'm a perspiring one.

On Sunday I went to Mass with Maria and Joe. I was impressed by their new priest, Father Tony. His homily inspired me. Two points I remember clearly. *Those who have gone before are still with us.* This remains, as part of the Catholic tradition, a tradition I live out in my regular chats with Maris. My belief in her ongoing presence sustains me. Never a day passes that I do not think of her. His second point was that we need to take care of ourselves, of our personal needs in order to be effective in living out our call. I found this piece of wisdom an unexpected bonus of my trip up north.

On the way back, I travelled inland along the New England Highway with the same routine. Travelling south on the way to Muswellbrook, I received an excited call from Angela. Her friend in Lennox Head was hearing my Lismore interview at that very moment.

My next tour was to Wollongong just a few days later.

I spent a weekend early February with my Family Group from St Anthony's at Gerringong. It was our practice to go away together about once a year. We stayed in a large house owned by the Christian Brothers, ideal for housing groups. There were twenty of us. On the Friday I visited bookshops in Wollongong and had an interview with the local newspaper and the ABC.

Back at the house I was very conscious that I was one of the solos. I had stayed at Gerringong in the past with Maris. I missed her and the things we did together. I visited the craft shops that she loved to visit and bought a bag for Jacinta. I took a trip on my own to the Benedictine Abbey at Jamberoo, one of Maris' favourite places. I bought some candles and prayed in the chapel, one of the most beautiful places I ever have ever visited. The ambience and atmosphere were extraordinary. The only sounds were the birds and a small fountain by the altar. An ideal place for meditation. I felt Maris' presence. This was one of her sacred places. I felt very close to her as I sat on my own as if I had somehow absorbed her spirit into my being and we were one again. I desperately wanted to join her, to be together just as we had been for forty-two years.

That evening, the family group had a meal and lots of drinks, with plenty of laughter and banter. Although I was in convivial and caring company I felt apart and had to fight the temptation to withdraw into myself.

On the Sunday morning, still under the spell of the chapel, I took a walk on my own along the cliff top. At one point the cliff was clear of bushes and as I looked down I thought of Maris and how she felt as she was falling. What thoughts were racing through her mind? What was her last thought?

I wanted to step back but I felt powerless as if I wanted to fall, too. I was held to the spot, far too close to the edge, looking down the endless waves crashing their spray against the cliff face.

What would happen if I fell? If I let my body go limp? The idea seemed almost attractive. I seemed to lose my fear of death. I'm not sure how long I stood there in silence. I was in a kind of trance, one part of me wanting to step forward. Then a thought seemed to seep into my mind as if someone was whispering into my ear. I'd like to think it was Maris.

'Noel, you'll mess up the family group weekend if you jump.'

I made a decision to rejoin the Family group for lunch and to return to life. That night back home, I reflected on the sensation I felt on top of the cliff. I think I gained a glimpse of what went through Maris' mind as she stood on the car park roof. I had dreams of jumping off that cliff, further reinforcement of the experts' comments that those bereaved by suicide are themselves a high risk group.

* * *

I reckoned that as my novel was set around Swan Hill, rural Victoria could be a good market. Country people would identify with the struggles of my fictitious community to keep their school open. So I headed to Melbourne for a grand promotional tour of the western half of Victoria. I stayed with Tim.

That night I received a call from an excited Angela. A review of my book had appeared in the *Sydney Morning*

Herald that morning. Jacinta rang shortly after with the same news.

'They've rubbished some of the other books but yours is good, Dad.'

I was elated. For the *Sydney Morning Herald*, which probably received hundreds of books per week, to have selected my book made me feel like I had arrived. I'd been recognised as serious enough a writer to have been considered worth reviewing. I was bursting with pride. Would that Maris were with me to share this joy.

I took two weeks for my book tour, calling on bookshops and seeking interviews with the local newspapers and radio stations. Back in Melbourne I rested with my brother Tom and his wife Robyn. The *Age* newspaper was full of a tragic accident at Mildura where a number of teenagers were killed. It occurred to me that the media would soon forget and go on to other events but the families would never forget. There was an article entitled 'The Myth of Closure' by Garry Tippet. Its theme: there is no such thing as closure. I thought of my own situation. I will carry Maris inside me for ever. I don't want to let go. I would not want it any other way. I'm on a journey I'll be taking for the rest of my life. I'm learning to cope but that doesn't mean closure. I'm just getting used to the idea that Maris is not around. There's no prescription that fits everyone on how to grieve. Selling my book is my way. Grieving has given me a tremendous energy. It changed me. It's as if I no longer dwell in the place I thought I did, but another where the familiar props of my life have been rearranged. Someone has entered my house, altered the rooms, replaced the carpet and shifted the furniture.

I probably spent more money promoting my book than

the amount I received from the sales. If I wanted to make money I would be doing other things, but I was satisfying other needs. I was maintaining a focus, keeping busy, ensuring that everyone who read my book would know of Maris.

She will not be forgotten, my Maris. While copies of my book are about, whether on people's bookshelves or gathering dust in bookshops, as soon as someone opens the pages, Maris' memory will spring into life.

CHAPTER 19

Dear Jacinta, Noel and family,
I must be one of so many who loved, admired and
really enjoyed Maris. She gave her kindness and caring
support so generously and freely to everyone and I some-
times wished that I worked a day shift instead of nights
to enjoy and share more of her fun and wisdom.
    Vaun

Revisiting France had been at the back of my mind since I was in Paris. I chose a language school in Chambéry, starting 1st July.
I discovered a writers' conference would be held end of June at the University of Winchester. Why not go? The timing was good. The details of a round-the-world trip evolved. I would fly to San Francisco, visit Rick's parents in Oregon, spend a few days in San Francisco and New York then fly to London and to Winchester, departing for Paris and finally Chambéry. It would be a five month trip in total.

I had a busy few months before taking off. I gained enormous benefit from a Lifeline in-service training residential weekend on bereavement. Saturday saw an illuminating presentation by Mal MacKissock, a guru in bereavement counselling. He discussed the helplessness one feels with the bereaved. His basic thought was that grief is an individual affair. If you don't feel helpless with a bereaved client, you've lost your humility and empathy. He dismissed many myths about grief and challenged much of the language used. He queried the concept of stages of grief as if it were sequential and predictable. He considered the best theory was chaos theory. Chaos is persistently unstable, like walking through a maze which rearranges itself as you pass through. My summary does not do justice to the day's richness.

On Sunday we had a religious service. I was asked to deliver a short homily. I talked about the impact Maris' death had on my life, but more about the positives. What was positive about Maris' death? The idea seemed indecent at first. But I reflected. In parting, Maris had given me a gift. I had experienced a profound sadness, like a passion, which, although it depressed me from time to time, had released an enormous amount of energy, an enthusiasm for life which had me criss-crossing the country. This same energy had me reaching out through Lifeline to others in crisis and walking with them in their suffering. I had rediscovered the simple truth that happiness is found in helping others.

Back home, Maris' influence pervaded my life. By now I had established three shrines, each complete with photo and candle, in the lounge room, in the family room and our bedroom. Her clothes still hung in the cupboard. Her handwriting was everywhere — in the address and telephone numbers book, her recipe box. Jacinta would use Maris' words when disciplining my grandson. Maris' presence was everywhere in the house, not as a ghost or spirit, but in a dimension of life beyond my comprehension. She was my partner, still is, albeit a silent one. I had interred my Maris in a grave, but I had also buried her in my heart.

I knew one day I would write about life post Maris, but not yet. I was not ready. It would be too painful. However, to support such a project, it seemed a good idea to apply for a literary grant from the Australia Council, and, on checking the website, wading my way through an extraordinary bureaucratic list of 'musts', I found that applications had to be received in May and the decisions would be announced in October. That fitted in with my trip. The Australia Council wanted a sample. So I sat down at my computer and wrote the first three chapters of this book. An unknown author, I did not have high expectations of a grant, but I could only try.

In writing those chapters, I recalled with great clarity her last month as I watched her sink deeper into her depression. Her pervasive feeling of sadness, a sense of life without joy, a feeling of impending catastrophe, the depression darkening her every moment. She had difficulty motivating herself to do anything. Many days she spent reading although I'm not sure her concentration was good. When she wanted to talk I would drop everything to sit with her, to be with her and to listen.

I found the experience of reliving the day of Maris' suicide exhausting. I was drained, relieved to place the submission in an envelope, post it and forget about it until I returned to Australia.

* * *

The family had another trip to Melbourne, this time for Tim's 30th birthday. Tim rang about ten days before.

'Dad, I'm planning to propose to Mel during the party,' he said.

'That's great, Tim,' I replied. 'The girls are always asking when's Tim going to declare himself.'

'I'm swearing you to secrecy, Dad.'

'Fine. It'll be hard, but I'll manage.'

In Melbourne we stayed with my brother Tom. On Saturday I walked from Tom's to the local shops to buy champagne to celebrate Tim and Mel's engagement announcement. Out of the blue in those quiet, sedate and leafy Mount Waverley streets, I had a major wallop. Tim's engagement would be a significant family event and Maris would not be present. I staggered back in tears. As I couldn't mention the secret, I had to find another explanation for my emotion, such as Tim turning thirty. That was sufficient. Most people born with Tim's medical condition do not survive childhood. The family knew that Maris' diligent nursing care enabled him to cope with his many childhood illnesses, and here he was, leaving his twenties a healthy adult.

The birthday party was a dress up affair. I went as Batman going to dinner, wearing my dinner suit and a Batman mask borrowed from Hughie. Angela and Jacinta were the Abba girls, Rick was Steve Irwin. After the cake was cut, Tim got on his knees and proposed. Mel's tears were taken as an acceptance. If ever there's a way to kick on a party (which was going pretty well anyway), it's somebody proposing in the middle of it. It's like pouring petrol on a fire. It was a late night and very emotional and joyous. The girls were crooked on me for not sharing the secret. In the midst of the hilarity, I managed a chat in a quiet corner with Mel's mother, Betty. She had lost her husband and we compared notes on being without a partner, particularly on such a joy-ous family occasion.

One of the Catenians, Jim, died. As a brother Catenian I attended his funeral and formed part of the guard of honour as the hearse left the church. I was happy to return the ser-vice to the Catenians who had formed the guard of honour at Maris' funeral. The Catenians continued to care for me. The newly installed President Gary invited me to dinner. Present were two other brothers who were without partners. We fell to discussing our situations. Ken's marriage had broken up and he did not want to repeat his mistake. Bruce, whose wife had died, considered there was no one else. I felt the same. No one could replace Maris.

* * *

My French visa arrived. I realised I was really going.

People were intrigued when I told them I was going to France to learn French. Why? they asked. Why not? I replied.

I had, scarcely articulate at first, a notion that there was a deeper meaning behind my trip. I was operating on two levels. On the surface I was travelling far and visiting vari-ous countries but at another level I was going deep into my interior. I was restless, impelled to go on a spiritual journey, a pilgrimage, a quest searching for I did not know what, an elusive dream, like reaching out to grasp the essence but your hands go through a shadow. I was freeing myself from the clock and the calendar, and all other responsibility. Other people sit on a mountain or the beach, trek in the desert or in Nepal. The French course was my retreat.

I was throwing myself into an activity removed from my normal life and seeing what emerged. What happened on my trip would probably profoundly change me and have an important bearing on the rest of my life. I wondered about my desire for adventure, for new ideas, for encountering the unknown, for living on the edge. I seemed to have an emotional need to reach out for what was beyond me. I'd like to think that, despite my age, I still had the glint of adventure in my eyes.

I was excited and enthusiastic, but I would have swapped everything — everything — to have Maris back.

I looked over her clothes. I knew I should do something about them before I left but I was still reluctant. I could manage to donate her work clothes to Lifeline. Sorting through them I found notes in her pockets. Messages about patients, reminders, notes for her colleagues. She loved her aged patients and often told me stories of the old demented chap who was once a plumber and regularly took the toilets apart or the fragile lady who was so tiny the wind blew her over. How I had missed those stories. It was bizarre coming across evidence of a part of her life I didn't know much about. A job which should have taken minutes seemed to take all day.

I couldn't touch her suits and dresses. I left her exercise books, too. They could wait until my return.

On our forty-third wedding anniversary I visited the cemetery and stayed for hours. I spent a lot of time talking about our forty three years together. Like any couple, we had our joys and our crises. Our major joy was our children. How fortunate was our decision to have four, considered a large family these days. Sitting on that bench I told Maris I still had ideas of joining her and occasionally as a truck thundered past me as I rode my bike I thought of an easy way. But I could still feel her saying, 'Not yet, Noel.'

Another major wallop came on Tessa's First Communion. The church was full of loving parents and doting grandparents, their eyes fixed on their own child. As I watched Tessa on the altar, beautifully dressed in white with white orchids in the hair, the tears flowed. This was a family event Maris would have hated missing — the first First Communion of our grandchildren.

Angela saw my tears. 'Dad, don't start me off,' she said. 'I've got to do a reading.' She maintained composure, read beautifully and kept her own tears for later.

'I still have my "rat shit" days,' I said to Angela afterwards.

'I have my rat shit days, too, Dad,' she told me, 'particularly when I go to a function and see happy grandmothers fussing around their families.'

On Mother's Day I debated whether I would go to church. St Anthony's always made a fuss of mothers, giving them flowers and inviting them to come forward to the altar. They would read a poem about mothers. I did go to Mass, feeling very alone and thinking Maris should be in the file of women, joking with her friends. A father and his twin toddlers handed out flower cards. The boys, a little overwhelmed at first, entered into their task with enthusiasm. I took three, for the three mothers in my family — Maris, Angela and Jacinta.

I contrasted my reaction on Mother's Day to that on Tessa's First Communion. I took Mother's Day calmly in my stride because I was prepared and expecting a reaction. In contrast, Tessa's First Communion overwhelmed me. It seems that if you expect to get walloped, it doesn't happen.

I had avoided Chatswood, particularly Chatswood Chase. I could not face the scene of Maris' death. On a visit to Sydney Stephen had bought a memory card. It was the wrong kind and he asked me to exchange it, a difficult task for him as he lived in Tamworth. It was unnerving to drive into the Westfield car park and recall that Maris had told me she considered taking her life here but had chosen Chatswood Chase instead. No way was I prepared to park at Chatswood Chase. At Westfield Shopping Centre, as I looked down on the central court, I was fragile. I felt weak in the legs, but different from the day I stood on the cliff at Gerringong. That day I was fascinated and death seemed almost attractive, but this day a fear gripped me somewhere deep inside as if a demon had invaded some inner sanctum of my life and vandalised its treasures.

I gained one benefit, however, when I visited one of the bookshops. On the bargain table I found a copy of *Men after Separation* by Ian Macdonald. I could identify with the men's stories and appreciate the dismay that forced them to extremes such as alcohol misuse and womanising. Reading their stories made me reflect on my own situation. Everyone does it differently. Although I felt like a vagabond, I was not completely rudderless. I had some inner and external resources to draw on in trying to create a new life, but, like the men in the book, I had many questions to face.

CHAPTER 20

Dear Noel,
Not a day goes by that I do not think of and remember
Maris, you and all your family. I see her kind face every-
where and feel she will walk down the drive into Grace
Cottage any day. It has been a privilege to know her
at least a little and her loving, gentle ways will remain
with me always.
  Barbara

Before Angela, Jacinta and I left for the airport I
checked Maris' tree. It was about three metres
tall, suspiciously like the tall peppermint gum
growing a few metres away.

'You should cut it down before it becomes a menace,'
Jacinta reminded me.

At the departure gates, amid tears and advice, Angela
gave me a card. Inside was a small Guardian Angel pin. A
small wallop: how fortunate I am to have two such beautiful,
caring daughters. Maris would be proud of them watching
over me.

On the flights to San Francisco, I felt alone, defence-
less even, as if I was about to step upon a frozen river with

all my normal supports missing. I chatted quietly to Maris. How would I handle myself if the ice became too thin and I had nowhere to go except into the water? I'd like to think it was Maris that reminded me of my formula — meet all my challenges with Cs rather than Ss. The voice that I heard was that of practical, pragmatic and rational Maris whom I knew and loved over so many years, not the Maris of her last few months, who was wracked with anxiety and pain, whose thinking was so twisted by her anguish.

A question that nagged me as I waited for the commuter plane to Crescent City. How would Rick's parents receive me? But when I arrived I realised I had worried for nothing. Dick and Barbara were very welcoming. They met me at the airport and drove me to their home at Brookings, a familiar place from my visit the previous year.

Dick and Barbara looked after me but I still had time on my own. I walked the trails along the coast, one of the most beautiful in the world, enjoying the forests rolling down to the rugged cliffs. I was told to look out for the 'cats'. I didn't meet any bob cats, cougars or mountain lions but I could hear the sea lions from the house and on two occasions went looking for them. On the first occasion, I told Barbara I'd be back in an hour, but underestimated the time it would take to scramble up and down cliffs. I arrived home two hours late. Barbara was frantic and ready to call the local rescue service. On another occasion, the wind blew my cap — complete with Angela's guardian angel — over the cliff. I gingerly climbed down to retrieve it.

Once I found myself on a beautiful, wild stretch of sand littered with rocks and driftwood. As I sat on a log watching the waves crash over the rocks, I had a major wallop. I ran down the beach and threw stones into the sea. 'You should be here, Maris,' I yelled over the roar of falling water. I seemed to hear her voice among the dim. 'I am,' she was saying. I calmed down and walked back to my backpack. I bent down and noticed a small piece of driftwood with an indent in the shape of a heart. If I made a cross of this, I thought, it would be a perfect symbol of love and a constant reminder of Maris' presence. I found a cross piece. I told Dick and Barb and the project became a family concern. With her craft work paint Barb added a slight touch of colour to the heart. Dick filed a slot two thirds of the way up the longer piece and glued the cross piece. The cross piece was a little off centre, the wood was rough at the ends. It would not have suited a perfectionist. For me, it was perfect.

The cross is an important spiritual tool. It fits beautifully into my hand. I hold it each morning and experience a sense of peace, timelessness and a connection with the infinite. Who knows how long those pieces had been lying on the beach, where they came from and how old was the original tree. My wooden cross is as important to me as my cross and chain.

At the Brookings bookstore I found a series of cards with dainty paintings of flowers and messages of inspiration. It was a quote by Albert Camus that had the biggest impact. *'In the midst of my darkness, I found the sun within myself.'*

Leaving Brookings was difficult as I had been made so welcome and had gained some insights into life in a small American town. On my day of departure Barbara drove me to the Crescent City airport. The plane for San Francisco was three hours late but the travellers were patient and many people knew each other. Even the security staff were relaxed and chatty. I noticed a young man who was concerned about an older lady confused by the delay. He helped her through security. He reminded me of Stephen at that age. He had a mass of curly hair and I tipped him as a caring person. We chatted. Mathew was from Santa Cruz, visiting Oregon to look at a possible college but was departing for France and Switzerland in five weeks time on his first solo European trip.

When the plane eventually arrived we sat together and exchanged a few confidences. He mentioned his depression when younger and I told him my story. He connected the reason for my travelling to Maris' death. It's amazing how close one can get to a complete stranger. Here I was, a 73 year old, confiding in a 19 year old, and he, in turn, confiding in me. The age difference didn't seem to matter.

In San Francisco, Mathew accompanied me on the BART train to downtown. He was familiar with the system and helped a fellow passenger find his right station. As we parted I gave him a copy of *Friend and Philosopher* and suggested that if he found Chambéry during his travels there would be space for him on the floor in my little apartment.

I had met Jean and Gail, friends of Barbara, the previous year while they were visiting Brookings. Barbara had arranged for them to look after me during my visit to San Fran. I wanted to visit Grace Cathedral because of its labyrinth floor tapestry, based on the medieval pavement design at Chartres Cathedral in France. The ancient practice of walking the labyrinth was revised in California in 1991. Its single-path design represents the journey of the spirit. It is a path of prayer and reflection, walked for spiritual insight and healing. Jean and Gail were happy to take me.

Jean, Gail and I finished looking around with morning tea and a chat. Both women were widows. We shared our experiences of life without a partner. They left me at the Grace Cathedral with invitations to return.

I approached the Cathedral as a tourist and as a pilgrim. I was unfamiliar with the labyrinth and was interested in this new way of prayer, to walk the pattern and allow the experience to seep into my spirit. I walked the path both inside and outside. At the bookshop, I bought *Praying the Labyrinth*. The author, Jill Kimberley Hartwell Geoffrion, describes her pilgrimage to Chartres Cathedral. Her book is a series of reflections as a result of walking the medieval labyrinth. I resolved that as I was visiting France, I, too, would walk that labyrinth.

* * *

To pass the time on the way to New York, I read *Praying the Labyrinth*. It gave me a lot of insights. It put into words what I was feeling. At one level, I was travelling around the world and learning French, but at another level, I was on a deeply personal journey, which was more than my reaction to Maris' death, more than working my way through the grieving process. High above the land mass of America I asked myself why was I going on this trip, this pilgrimage? I sensed a profound longing. For what? I asked. I couldn't explain. I didn't know yet. I was hoping that I would find out later. For the moment I had to trust. I had to be who I was, to remain open, to be receptive, to accept all the challenges and to grow with each experience. I recalled the scouting advice we gave each other when bushwalking: 'Don't get so caught up climbing to the top the mountain that you miss appreciating the view on the way.'

This time in NYC I was staying at the YMCA. I was selective in what I wanted to see and do. I went to the Lincoln Centre, checked out the shows and bought tickets. I paid for good seats, reasoning that I had saved money by staying in budget accommodation. I wandered about the Centre, an interesting concentration of theatres. In the afternoon I walked around Central Park. Last time it was covered in snow but that day it was bathed in a very warm sun. Very much a park for the people, numerous activities crowded its streets and lawns — cycling, skate boarding, walking, strolling, jogging, busking, sun bathing, riding in rickshaws pulled by cyclists, horse drawn carriages, fun parks, even a wedding. Although people were trying to relax, there seemed a high degree of intensity in all the activity, a parallel to the frenzied pace of New York. Descriptions of Central Park as the lungs of New York were very appropriate.

In the evening I went to the New York City Ballet at the New York State Theatre which boasted a spectacular foyer. The programme consisted of three pieces — Divertimento (sweet and gracious), Episodes (jerky but it came good) and Vienna Waltzes (very lush). The lady next to me was a regular who had seen just about everything the company had staged.

The next day started with a walk down Broadway to 51st Street and along to St Patrick's Cathedral. Unlike the year before, this time when I lit a candle for Maris I was calmer. A funeral Mass was underway. I listened to a lady delivering a eulogy on her twin sister. I walked down the isle to receive Communion but a security guard stopped me saying this was a private Mass. I could go to Communion at the mid-day Mass. This was a shock. He was theologically incorrect because there is no such thing as a private Mass as the Table of the Lord is open to all. Here was another wallop. I wasn't prepared to argue with this burly, black man. Even though I knew Jesus accepted me and that it was the humans who ran this show that had got it wrong, I felt lonely and rejected. The ice was getting thin.

That night I saw *The Light in the Piazza*, a musical about Americans in Italy. The music was wonderfully romantic but the story was sentimental and silly. The lady sitting next to me had come with her daughter from Chicago just to see the show. The next day I attended the matinee of the American Ballet's *Giselle*. The music and dancing were excellent but, like the *Light on the Piazza*, the story was silly. The snooty ladies next to me didn't want to know me.

Maris and I attended the theatre frequently. We tried to make the Opera House at least once a year and subscribed to the Glen Street Theatre and the Marion Street Theatre. Our last night out together was at the Opera House, three days before she died. In Sydney I would have had difficulty in attending the theatre without thinking of the many pleasant nights we shared. I would not have gone without feeling an immense sense of loss. Yet here in New York City I was happy to go on my own, not once but three times.

I spent my last morning in America first at the 8 am Mass at St Paul the Apostle, just around the corner from the YMCA. It was Father's Day and I was happy to receive a blessing along with the other dads. I spent the rest of the morning sitting in a sunny Central Park while waiting for the airport shuttle bus. What a passing parade of strollers, skaters, dog walkers, joggers, cyclists, horse drawn carriages and rickshaws! The park was full with the joy of life. It should have been contagious and I should have been happy, surrounded by all this positive energy. Instead, I felt a touch of sadness as I thought of Maris. Her depression prevented her from enjoying life, from being 'fully alive'. Her pain was so great she sought death. To have her back to enjoy this scene...

On the airport shuttle someone had written 'Beloved Karen, Make me immortal with a kiss, David' on the back of the seat in front of me. I was tempted to add my own version underneath but wrote in my journal instead.

CHAPTER 21

*Beloved Maris, Would that I could make you mortal
with a kiss. Noel*

Once in London, I was keen to see St Paul's
again. My visit the year before was a highlight. This time, I found the same prayerful
atmosphere, despite the larger crowd. I lit a candle for Maris
again in St Dunstan's chapel and reflected on the meaning of
that candle using the same card as last year. *(See page 115)*

As I read and reread that card, I asked myself if it held a key.
Could I regard myself as a candle giving light to myself and
others? Could I aim to reach out to others, giving warmth,
hope and love? I was on a pilgrimage, an interior journey.
I was having a rendezvous with myself or, rather, with that
person I always believed to be me. Would I find a familiar
person or a different man? I was trying to be true to myself.
Where my journey was leading, I had no idea. In the midst
of my darkness, I might find the sun within myself.

I was restless. I was searching. Something was missing.
Certainly I was missing Maris, but my search had taken on
deeper spiritual dimensions. The word 'spiritual' suggests a
linking of all the different facets of one's life into one whole,

which gives a sense of meaning to that whole. Was I searching for meaning? Since losing Maris, I sometimes had a feeling that my life was going nowhere. I had filled my days with activities and focused on promoting my book, but there was still a void. Perhaps that is why I was finding the lighted candle such an important symbol, as holding a key to my quest, the link that brought my life together. It is difficult now in retrospect to put in some order the jumble of thoughts that tossed themselves around in my mind in this beautiful cathedral. I thought I had a glimmer of insight. Perhaps the feelings were more important than the thoughts. I certainly experienced a feeling of hope. It was Pope Benedict XVI that said, 'Whoever has hope lives differently; a new life has already been given to him.' That made a lot of sense to me.

I sat for a long time in St Dunstan's chapel, in a kind of meditation, indifferent to the constant stream of curious visitors. I accepted an invitation to join the Eucharist at midday. Fifty or so people peeled off the mob of tourists and participated in a service not unlike the Catholic Mass.

I shed my pilgrim's cloak and donned my tourist cap as I climbed the 500 plus steps to the top of the dome to admire the magnificent views of London and the interior of the cathedral. An attendant gave me a blast for taking photos with a flash. I had to be more discreet. I returned to ground level. My candle was still burning. I lit another for Maris, and left them as prayers. I was reluctant to leave St Paul's but eventually walked out late afternoon, thinking I should continue the tourist thing and see some more of London.

The next morning I devoted to 'make and mend' activities. I found a laundrette. I had a hair cut. In the afternoon I attended the Victoria Palace Theatre for a performance of

Billy Elliot the Musical. The show deserved all its accolades. The dancing was spectacular and the story was powerful with plenty of political and emotional punch. The matinee audience was friendly and I chatted to people around me. They were interested in my Australian accent. All had their Australian story to tell.

Friday morning I took a bus to Winchester. I had visited Winchester with Maris in 2001 when I attended a conference of the British Psychological Society at the Guildhall. The writers' conference was held at the university. The twenty-sixth Winchester Writers' Conference brought together authors, playwrights, poets, producers, literary agents, commissioning editors and industry specialists. Through a series of mini courses, workshops, seminars, lectures and one-to-one appointments, participants had the opportunity to harness their creative ideas and to develop their technical and marketing skills.

I was not sure what I might gain from the conference. I was hoping to sell a few copies of *Friend and Philosopher* at the book fair held in conjunction. I was looking for creative input for my manuscript *Whistler Street*. I was in the final stages of fine-tuning, working my way through word by word, constantly changing and rewriting.

I was looking for ideas to develop this project. My previous efforts were in fiction but I was embarking on a new genre in writing autobiography, a very different proposition. The more ideas, the better. I attended a workshop 'Turning your Life into Literature'. It was okay but the work shop leader had no qualms about plugging her own works.

I imagined the British novice writer has the same struggle as the Australian to get his or her book published. I was looking forward to exchanging views. My experience of attending conferences is that you gain more in the breaks and the bars talking to the other participants than from the formal sessions. Winchester was no different. There were about 400 conferees and I spoke to so many people — in the bar and over meals — all with the same interest in writing. Many were interested in my Australian accent.

'Have you come all this way just for the conference?'

I had to admit I was on my way to France.

We were allowed three one-to-one meetings. Two of them were with established writers with whom I discussed creative issues. Then I met with James, who was employed in a publishing agency. He had long hair and a hat perched on the back of his head and looked like a younger version of the British spiv. He had good credentials, having read English Literature at Edinburgh University. I told him about my plan to write an account of my journey.

'Ah, what the trade calls a misery memoir,' he said. Then he added, 'But they sell.'

The conference organisation was homely rather than slick. The atmosphere was relaxed and welcoming. The conference took its tone from the organiser, Barbara Large, who was a member of the faculty and had organised the conference for many years. I imagined her to be a high-powered female executive and was pleasantly surprised to meet a friendly, warm, grandmotherly figure, with a great interest in all the participants and a passion for writing.

'Keep on writing,' was her constant motto.

Most of the participants went home Sunday afternoon but about forty stayed on for the rest of the week. We were taken by bus to Southdown, a small village about five miles out of

Winchester. My hosts Maria and Richard weren't really in the bed and breakfast trade, but helping out Barbara who happened to be a neighbour. Maria was Italian and very anxious to please. John's clipped manner of speech reminded me of the stiff Englishman, but he was warm and welcoming underneath. My fellow guest was John from Stirling, Scotland. A larger than life character with a beard, big stomach and red face, which reminded me of Falstaff, he was a retired Presbyterian minister and lived in a castle.

The title of the five day workshop was 'Creating, Writing, Revising and Marketing Your Fiction'. We were a group of six. We spent the time writing, reading, listening to and commenting on each others' work. John was in my group along with Mark who lived in Belgium but was born in South Africa. He spoke English, Afrikaans and French. Marian was quiet and timid. She lived on the Isle of Wight. She used language beautifully but lacked confidence. Susan was also quiet. She was a retired lexicographer. In contrast, Clare was a loud, bright, outgoing English woman, married to a Moroccan, and lived in Morocco.

That week was memorable. After spending the days in session at the local village hall, we met each evening with the participants from other classes and walked in the summer twilight along tow paths originally laid by the Romans. Then at about 9 pm we stopped for dinner at a traditional English pub, before walking back to our accommodation about midnight. How I wished Maris was with me. She would have enjoyed those balmy summer evenings and the conversation. She would have talked about family, and sooner or later the others would have revealed their hearts to her.

Our last night was nostalgic. By that time we had built up

quite a rapport with like-minded people, all of whom were trying to turn a dream into a reality. We exchanged confidences. I told them my story and about my intended visit to France. Mark gave me tips about living in France. He taught me some street French (such as 'ça se laisse boire', which means roughly 'this drink's going down well'). I sold more books. I received encouragement to follow my intention to write about my journey. When I mentioned they would be included, they demanded to be sent copies. Barbara came on these walks. She was a generous soul, interested in me as the conferee who had come from across the world. She knew suffering herself, having lost a husband and a son.

The conference was a week of inspiration but, like most conferences I gained more from the ambience and the interchange than from the lecture content.

CHAPTER 22

My pain gives me an opportunity for growth.
— Maris' journal, December, 2001

I spent one night in Paris at the Hotel Corail because it was near the Gare de Lyon. As I lay in my bed, drifting into sleep to the sounds of the Paris traffic, I checked out the last month. I was thankful this was my last night of travelling for a while. The worst part of being on the move is dragging your luggage up and down flights of stairs. I tried to travel light with two bags, and I noticed they were small in comparison to other travellers. I was looking forward to staying in one spot, to my three months at Chambéry. On the way to Paris, I'd been touched by anxiety a few times but everything seemed to work out.

Sometimes, I felt impatient to get to Chambéry, but I had to remind myself to value every experience, every moment as I was in 'time out' with my normal life suspended.

I laughed at the word 'normal'. The thought of a 'normal life' sent me travelling back over the last eighteen months. Maris' suicide had shaken up all my assumptions about life and what is normal. My 'normal life' back in Sydney was nowhere near what it was, say, two years before. Back then I used to have a good idea of who I was and how I functioned. I used to be one half of a couple. I used to think that Maris and I would grow old together and that together we would make decisions about our future. I used to think we would continue together with our overseas travel.

Now the security I felt in the world had been challenged. Nothing was predictable. The pattern of my life had been turned upside down. No longer one of a couple, I was just one. I had become a kind of restless vagabond who had travelled across the world to find himself. Here I was, trying to get to sleep in the smallest of rooms in a budget hotel with the tiniest of showers. The journey that I was on was not about going back to how I was before, but of adjusting to the changes and coping with a life that I now saw very differently. On the surface, I would reach my destination when I took the train in the morning to Chambéry, but in my interior journey I was unsure where I was heading.

I managed to get some sleep and in no time it was Saturday morning and I was wandering around the cavernous exterior of the Gare de Lyon checking the departure schedules. Along with hundreds of other, I stared at the huge noticeboard, waiting for my platform number to be announced. I was even asked a few directions, so I must have looked part of the scene, just as Angela had advised over a year before.

I found my carriage without any trouble and as I sat in my seat I felt my total immersion had begun. I was surrounded by French conversation. I shared a few words with the lady next to me, who was intrigued I was Australian and had come so far. She was visiting her grandchildren. A lady with many bags sat opposite, but she was too immersed in keeping track of them to worry about chatting. As I sat back and watched the suburbs flash by, I was pleased that I had managed the process of getting myself on the train, from the planning to the actual travel. My train was a TGV (train à grande vitesse), a very fast train indeed. We picked up speed and moved swiftly through the French countryside. That mode of travel leaves car travel for dead.

As we neared Chambéry, a four hour trip, I was touched by anxiety about getting to my accommodation. I had to remind myself of my formula. I should meet all my challenges with Cs. My apprehension was stronger than usual. I asked Maris to look after me. Perhaps I was still grieving, calm on the surface but inwardly broken and unsure how the pieces should go back together.

I need not have worried. Jean-Charles met me at the station. He spoke very slowly, so unusual for a Frenchman, and repeated himself to make sure I understood everything.

He gave me a quick tour of the town and showed me the road I should walk along on Monday morning to get to the language school. He then took me to my accommodation in Rue de la République at the Résidence Curial. It looked like a hotel with a reception but all the rooms were apartments. I had a studio apartment on the third floor with small kitchenette and bathroom. The apartment was quite small, mind you, but that was not a problem as I felt I would be contained and during my stay in a better position to put my pieces together.

The weather was a scorcher. No air conditioning. I decided I would cook for myself so as soon as I had dumped my baggage, I went looking for a supermarket. I asked a few directions on the way, and people asked me directions. Angela would be pleased. I was already looking a local — an old bloke, shopping bag on his arm, doing his Saturday arvo shopping. I found a supermarket after a 15 minute walk. It took two trips. On the first visit I got into serious trouble with the check-out chick for not weighing my bananas. I explained in my best French that I was a visitor and didn't know the system. That made her grumpier. Finally, a kind gentleman in the queue grabbed my bananas and weighed them for me. Lots of 'merci beaucoup monsieur' followed. The check-out girl was pregnant and she was short with other customers, so I guess she was suffering from the heat. On my second visit, I made sure I weighed my fruit and vegetables. I even helped a lady weigh hers. She had no French and seemed very lost.

That night I cooked my first meal; a very Australian-style steak, egg and salad but with a bottle of French red wine. It was still very hot so I went out after dinner. There were many bars. Everyone was watching the Soccer World Cup game, France versus Brazil. I moved from bar to bar but stayed with one which had the television outside and some seats along the footpath. I stood at the back and became just as excited as the rest. I too yelled out 'Allez bleu' to encourage the French team and 'Asseyez' to blokes who kept standing and blocking the screen whenever there was excitement. The streets went mad when France won. Car horns blew all night.

I did some house keeping Sunday morning. I placed Maris' photo on the TV. I hung an Aussie flag on the wall and a Sydney Swans Calender in the kitchenette. I tried to do my washing. For a while I was very confused, losing my coins fast until I worked out that what I thought was the dryer was actually the washer and vice versa. I found the Cathedral for Mass at 11 am. I lit a candle for Maris and had a minor wallop.

'You should be here, Maris,' I whispered to her. 'You would love this beautiful, ancient town, steeped in history, surrounded by mountains.'

As I sat before the candle, it dawned on me I would never have taken this language course if Maris was still alive. I would never have come to Chambéry. Her death was my opportunity. The thought of gaining a benefit from my loss saddened me and threatened to send me spiralling into a guilt trip. I found myself saying sorry to Maris but I seemed to hear her say, 'Consider your trip to be a gift from me.'

At the cathedral I picked up a leaflet advertising a pilgrimage to Lourdes to be held in the first week of October. I was due to finish at the language school end of September. I had made no plans for October apart from a last few days in Paris. The timing was perfect.

Studies at the language school started each Monday. I chose July 3rd as enrolment day. So did quite a number of students judging by the crowd that took the written exam. The exam was easy. I liked the comprehension questions best. They indicated at least that I could read French. We did an individual oral test, so I rattled off a few phrases in my best French accent. While waiting I spoke to other students. I met a lad from Denmark, two ladies from Israel and an older man from Switzerland who had accompanied his granddaughter. We were to be told at 5.30 pm our results and class placement.

In the meantime, Jean-Charles lead us on a town walking tour, taking us into a labyrinth of ancient alleys and relating many stories in his slow, repetitive French. We visited the best known monument, the splendidly extravagant Fontaine des Elephants, created in 1838 to honour the Comte de Boigne whose chateau houses the language school. We also visited the Château des Ducs de Savoie, the former residence of the Savoy Dukes. On the walk, I met Jack, a quiet American from San Francisco. He was tall and slim. His hair was red and his face freckled. He told me he was a singer, almost thirty years old and a dysfunctional individual up to now. I was intrigued. He seemed an interesting person to get to know. At 5.30 pm they gave us champagne and put up the class lists ranging from Beginners to Advanced. To my surprise, my name was in the Advanced class. I knew more French than I thought.

Tuesday was the first day of classes. I found myself with twelve other students, only one male, most of whom I would have given a good fifty years. However, that didn't seem to matter as we got under way. I found their acceptance of me refreshing. We were all embarking on a similar adventure. Our teacher, Corinne, a small but confident lady, was very welcoming. She spent time addressing each student and getting them to tell their story. She found me intriguing, I think, being the eldest and from the other side of the world. I had to explain why I was studying French. She would not accept an answer such as 'Why not?' (Pourquoi pas?) She spoke very, very rapidly but her explanations were excellent and she went into considerable detail. I found the strain enormous, concentrating and listening intently to a foreign language, fearful I might miss an important instruction, with absolutely no English allowed. Harder still to express myself, stumbling to find the right words in my limited vocabulary, let alone getting the right tense, mood and conjugation. Corinne's standards were high. No chance of sitting back quietly and coasting. She used humour very well and chided us gently for our errors. She organised us into groups for exercises.

I worked with girls from Brazil, Japan and Russia. I was thankful for the end of the class. I'm certainly in this immersion business up to my neck, I thought to myself, but am I in over my head?

I was not feeling confident about the next class. I had to remind myself not to worry. It didn't really matter if I didn't do well apart from my pride. I kept reminding myself I wasn't doing this for sheep stations. Nothing of importance was hanging on my learning French. I should be enjoying myself, allowing things to roll along.

The school offered free access to the internet in a room full of computers, always crowded with students checking their emails. I checked mine, too, but had to adjust to the French keyboard. It was bizarre to find that what you had typed was not what you had written. Just a few letters in different places, enough to incur frustration. Eventually I found the missing letters. The apostrophe was the most elusive. I tracked it down among the numerals.

The family had written to keep me informed of the Sydney Swans progress through the season. One email was from Mathew, the young man I met at Crescent City. He was in Switzerland and looking for a bed in France. Could he visit me? Could I cope with a visitor as well, I thought. But then I heard Maris' voice saying, 'Reach out, Noel.'

'Certainly,' I typed.

* * *

By the end of the first week I was intellectually and emotionally exhausted. Along with both the novelty of the situation and the heat, I had difficulty sleeping. There was considerable noise outside my apartment. The square outside was an echo chamber but I had to keep the window open for the ventilation. I was relieved when Mathew emailed to say he would be delayed. I needed a little time on my own.

After one week was I any better with my French? If not, why the heck was I putting myself through this ordeal? Why not behave like other seventy-three year olds and go on a comfortable cruise where I could sit in a deckchair sipping a beer and listen to other oldies' detailed account of their health. But where was the adventure? Every experience, everything that happens and whatever I do are part of my journey. Nothing is a waste of time. I was thankful that my health and fitness enabled me to take on these challenges and survive.

I was pleased with my interactions with the community. When I developed dry eyes I visited a chemist, discussed my symptoms with the pharmacist and bought the appropriate product. When I needed a new pair of sneakers, I discussed size, style and colour happily and paid thirty-five euros. I learned the layout of the supermarket although I had to ask assistants. If I did not know the French name, I tried to explain its function. It was a delight to see the assistant's face light up when he or she understood what I wanted. I still had problems at the checkout hearing and understanding the price. It was a slow process, hearing the numerals in French, translating them into English and offering the right amount.

By the end of the second week, I was beginning to adapt.

Philippe was our second teacher. He was quiet, thoughtful, reflective and intellectual. He introduced us to the poetry of

Jacques Prévert. I found the poems very moving, yet so simple and I bought his book *Paroles*. I was particularly moved by a poem entitled *Le Message*. It reminded me of Maris. I asked Philippe for the name of a good modern author. He suggested Anna Gavalda; I bought one of her books. I was disappointed when Philippe announced he was with us for two weeks — a substitute during the summer vacations.

I met Mathew at the railway station. I hoped I would recognise him and that he hadn't cut his hair. I do not trust my memory for faces. I looked closely at every young man with bubbly black hair. I wasn't sure about one and asked if his name was Mathew. He said no (non!). A few minutes later he approached me and asked if I spoke English (Parlez-vous Anglais?) He explained in American English he was a student and waiting to be met by his host family and asked if I was that person. Eventually Mathew walked out of the station and there was no mistaking him — big smile, large nose and of course bubbly black hair. It was as if we had known each other for years. He reminded me again of Stephen.

Mathew stayed for four days. I found his youthful presence stimulating. What a delightful age, nineteen! Sometimes he acted the adult and we had serious conversation about his future and the place of America in the world. I teased him with questions about his perception of what the world thought of America now that he was in a foreign country and what was it like being a citizen of the most powerful country in the world. His comments were thoughtful and perceptive. He had developed his own philosophies of life which he was keen to share. His perception of me was that I was searching for peace and referred me to a certain maharaja and his web site. At other times, Mathew was a child — exuberant, full of self-assurance, almost arrogant, and enthusiastic about his travel experience. He did not have much French but he used it to full advantage in his exchanges with the locals. I admired his confidence. That night we watched the World Cup Final — France versus Italy — in the same bar as I watched France beat Brazil. We shouted 'Allez bleu' at the exciting moments and were disappointed along with the rest of France when Italy won after two periods of time out and a shoot-out. The town was quiet that night.

Mathew left for Marseilles early one morning. I mentioned that if he decided to visit the Great South Land I would welcome him and provide a proper bed, not the floor. He was not backwards in offering advice and as we walked down the passageway to the lift, loaded with his backpack, he turned to me and said, 'Noel, don't be afraid to step out of your boundaries.'

'I reckon I'm doing that already.'

CHAPTER 23

You can't tell me worry doesn't do any good. What I worry about never happens.
— From a card purchased at the bookshop in Brookings

I began to wonder if I had been put in the right class. As I settled into sleep one night, I thought of Maris and put the question to her.

'Should I approach the François Principal and ask to be regraded?'

'What for?' I thought I heard her voice in the rustle of the curtains.

'I'm happy enough with my reading, writing and comprehension but conversation's my weakness. In our class discussions, I want to be fluent, of course, but I have to think intently about what I want to say. By the time I've worked out vocabulary, the gender of the noun, the tense of the verb, etc., I've lost fluency.'

'You've compared yourself with the fluent,' she seemed to reply, whispering in the dark. 'Don't forget you're among serious students, still at University in their home countries, used to sitting in classes while you haven't sat in a classroom for decades.'

I knew she was right. 'I'm beginning to think I'm in the advanced class under false pretences.'

'Have you talked to the other students?' her gentle voice seemed to ask.

'Yes. A lot of them are struggling much as I am. I've talked to students who've been promoted. They complained to François of being bored because the level was too simple for them. Perhaps I'm at the right level, after all, difficult as it is.'

Maris seemed to go silent, as if I knew what I should do.

'Okay, I'll stay and tough it out.' My last thought as I drifted off to sleep was 'It's better to be challenged than to be bored.'

I met students from other classes. They came from everywhere — Britain, USA, Spain, Italy, Germany, Switzerland, Holland, Denmark, Russia, Egypt, Israel, Saudi Arabia, Japan, China, Malaysia, Brazil, Columbia, Czech Republic. Their reasons for studying French were mixed. A few were 'tourists'. They stayed a week or two, as part of a summer holiday to freshen up their French or learn a few handy phrases before their travels. The more serious students stayed longer, from one month up to a year or more. Apart from the university students, there were doctors from middle-east countries hoping to specialise in French hospitals. A Chinese girl was planning to study music in Paris. Two Russian girls (very beautiful) were hoping to break into the French fashion model world. Missionaries were learning French before taking up posts in former French colonies in Africa. Columbian students just out of school were planning to pursue tertiary studies in French universities. Then there were the lost souls, me included, studying for no particular career reason, endeavouring to find themselves after some personal loss.

Jack, the quiet American, was among the lost souls. We had a long lunch together on an unexciting Bastille Day. He chose a small outdoor restaurant specialising in pasta in the shadow of the cathedral. Over the course of the afternoon, we told each other our story. He was finding himself studying French after a broken relationship. Jack was raised in San Francisco. He rejected his parents' fundamentalist religious training and moved to the fringes of the music world where he had made a number of recordings. He promised to give me one.

'You don't look a rock singer to me, Jack,' I joked, relaxed after a couple of glasses of wine.

'How come?'

'Your hair's too short; your manner's too gentle. I can imagine you, though, leaning your tall slim figure into a guitar.'

Now at the age of twenty-nine he was struggling to find maturity. He had been a travelling vagabond and would like to remain one but knew he had to settle down and find a job to support his singing. He was working on another recording.

'We're both aspiring artists, Jack. You as a musician and me as a writer.' I promised to give him a copy of *Friend and Philosopher.*

Jack found the Australian idiom colourful. He was intrigued at some of the expressions I used and I had to explain what they meant. Not playing for sheep stations took some explaining. We walked back to his bicycle chained to a fence near the Elephant Fountain. In fumbling to unlock the padlock, Jack dropped his keys down a drain but managed to retrieve them with a stick which I, hoping the police were taking the holiday, had ripped off one of the trees.

We formed a bond that dull Bastille Day afternoon, over our pasta and white wine, thrown together in our searching for something.

'You're endeavouring to stop being a vagabond, Jack, and I'm trying to become one.' I said in the shade of the Elephant Fountain. That day cemented our friendship. We became good mates and often met after class for a drink.

I'm old-fashioned enough to believe that although emails have their place in this modern electronic world, people enjoy receiving postcards. On our earlier overseas trips, Maris wrote all the postcards. I spent the rest of Bastille Day preparing a list from my address book. I wanted to keep in touch with everyone back in Australia in the way Maris used to, and by evening I had developed a list of about seventy names. I was to write four or five each day for the next few weeks.

* * *

It was on an excursion to Lyon, arranged by the language school, that I palled up with Elaine. She was English and lived in Ireland. Together we followed Jean-Charles through the old city. Speaking in his slow French, he conducted us through a district named Presqu'Isle (almost an island), a narrow peninsular of land between the Rhône and Saône Rivers. He took us to the Basilique Notre-Dame, a gaudy mock-Byzantine creation built in the late 19th century, on top of the hill overlooking the town, then to a Roman theatre, the oldest in France, built in 15BC to seat 10,000, where they were rehearsing for a rock concert.

Elaine and I bought baguettes and had lunch together sitting in the gutter. We walked through a warren of cobbled streets and traboules (covered passageways) full of churches, restaurants and chic designer shops. A kids' shop impressed me. It had everything an aspiring mother or doting grand-mother would wish.

'My wife Maris would have bought half the stock for our grandchildren,' I told Elaine.

'Are you going to buy anything?' she asked.

'No. The prices take your breath away, even before you translate them to Aussie dollars. I'll find a kids' shop back in Chambéry with more reasonable prices.'

We sat together in the bus on the way back and had a recovery drink at the Café Théâtre, which was to become my favourite bar. I felt comfortable with Elaine. We spoke about our families and our stories. Elaine, too, was a lost soul, recovering from a bitter divorce. She had two sons in their twenties and an after-thought daughter aged ten who lived with the father. I was to see a lot of Elaine.

On Sunday I attended the 11 am Mass as I did nearly every Sunday during my stay. The cathedral was rather ugly. The proportions were wrong. The roof wasn't high enough and it didn't have the soaring effect the great cathedrals have. There was always a gauntlet of regular beggars outside, hands outstretched wishing me 'Bonne Messe' (Have a good Mass). I usually gave a coin or two, which was greeted by obsequi-ous mutterings and bowing. Once inside, I enjoyed the Mass. By now, I had found the bookshop where they sold *Prions en Eglise* (Let us pray in church), a booklet containing the liturgy for the month. I was able to follow the readings and as the homily was usually based on them, I had a good chance of following and getting a message. I was pleased with myself because I was learning the order of the Mass in French.

As well as offering some spiritual solace, church attendance was a French lesson in itself. The singing was excellent. The choir consisted of four tenors whose voices blended so beautifully it was worth going to church just to listen to them.

That afternoon the weather was still very hot. I found myself in my non air-conditioned apartment sitting naked at my laptop. I took several showers in an effort to keep cool. I recalled a conversation with the two ladies from Israel. They said it was just as hot in their country but they had the benefit of air-conditioning and were looking to going back to escape the heat. They left the previous Friday just as the conflict between Israel and Lebanon began. Which was better I thought? Sweltering in Southern France or taking your chances on a Hezbollah rocket landing on the roof of your air conditioned house in Israel?

That evening, as on most evenings, I watched television. As part of my total immersion programme I looked at far more TV than at home. I actually enjoyed the quiz shows and followed a series of old Western films. It was quaint to see John Wayne in action on the French screen. Sometimes he spoke in his drawl with French sub-titles but other times he was dubbed. John Wayne speaking French just wasn't right. His voice was part of his character. On the other hand, speaking French really suited Clark Gable.

I supplemented the TV news with the newspaper *Le Figaro*. I'd skim the head lines and sit down with the dictionary when I wanted to read an article in depth. I enjoyed following the presidential campaign. The Socialist party was endeavouring to win the support of other left wing parties. The various candidates from the Socialist camp were jostling with each other for selection, although Nicholas Sarkozy seemed to be the most likely choice for the UMP. Because I was reading *Le Figaro*, a right wing newspaper, my source of information had a definite bias.

There wasn't much Australian news. The first was an article mentioning that John Howard, rather than stand down, had announced he would contest the next election as Prime Minister, much to the chagrin of Peter Costello whom the paper named Le Dauphin. Steve Irwin's death was well covered. The Australian women's hockey team beating Russia in the World Championships received coverage in the sports page. In the arts section I found an extensive review of Tim Winton's latest book, *The Turning*. In a series entitled Ordinary Heroes I read an article of a Central Australian aboriginal woman who successfully opposed the establishment of a nuclear waste dump in her country.

A new teacher replaced Philippe. Chantal was an older woman who stayed with us for two weeks. I enjoyed her fussy and pedantic approach. She was a stickler for pronunciation. Getting the correct pronunciation is a tricky business, particularly as many words are spelt the same in French and English. Not only was I pronouncing a word such as 'organisation' the English way, I was adding an Australian accent as well. She was quieter and less blustery than Corinne, but she believed firmly in class participation. One of her favoured exercises was to take articles from newspapers, break the class into small groups and give each group an article which they had to analyse, summarise and present to the class.

Chantal was intrigued by my presence. 'Why have you come all this way?' she asked me one day.

I told her some of my story and we became friends. I was sorry to see her go at the end of the month. I saw her around the town. She always greeted me warmly and was keen to chat.

I joined the school's excursion to the local vineyards. I gained knowledge of the local vintages, handy in buying wines from the supermarket. There is a long tradition of wine making in the region where they have been making wines since the Roman days. I was pleased Elaine had joined the excursion, I won't say I wasn't, and after the tour we once more shared a recovery drink at the Café Théâtre.

* * *

The 26th July was Maris' birthday. She would have been sixty-eight. Our family has always observed birthdays and from the earliest days of our marriage, we always got together to celebrate. Maris was the one to remember and organise a party. Now our children followed. They all contacted me. I spoke to Angela, Stephen and Tim. Jacinta sent a text message. So did my sister Maria.

I thought of Maris every day, but this day more so. I thought of the many family celebrations, the joyous times we had together. I thought of our forty-two years and the bed we had shared. I decided I should buy her a birthday gift. I already had her photograph on the television set. I would add a plant and candle and transform the TV top into a shrine.

I found a delightful garden shop with the name 'J'ai descendu dans mon jardin' (I've come down into my garden) just down the road. I selected a little pot plant with reddish leaves, the name of which I've forgotten. I knew it in French. The shop assistant found me a candle.

Back at the apartment, I arranged the photo, pot plant and

candle on the TV. I lit the candle and a fragrance filled the room. It reminded of the fragrance from the candle Maris sometimes lit at home during her meditations, just another means of her trying to rid herself of her depression. I wiped a tear away as I gazed at the photo, plant and candle. The shrine transformed the room. It seemed more like home, not just a temporary shelter. Some of the broken pieces were being put back together. I had acknowledged Maris' spirit and she was truly with me.

* * *

I was pleased as we came to the end of July, memorable for its heat. Every day the temperature stretched into the thirties. In contrast to Sydney's summer where a fresh southerly will disrupt the summer heat every few days, the heat of Chambéry was relentless. Day after day, without the benefit of an occasional cool change or air conditioning, the town baked under the sun. The nights brought little relief. The weather reports indicated that the rest of Western Europe was just as hot. The government declared a heat wave and issued health warnings. By the end of the month I was exhausted not only from the strain of learning French and the immersion in a different culture but from the inescapable heat.

'Why am I putting myself through this torture?' I found myself asking Maris, as I lay naked on the bed, trying to get some sleep. 'I'm losing confidence. I'm having a crisis. Should I pack up and go home, back to the family and familiar surroundings, back to a Sydney winter, mild by any standards? There had to be less masochistic ways to pass a European summer.'

'What about the other students?' I thought I heard Maris' voice stirring in the heavy, oppressive air.

'They're having as much difficulty. Some are physically sick and missing classes. At least I've gone every day, five days per week, four hours each day.'

'Have you been taking care?' I imagined the same chiding tone that I used to hear whenever Maris was discussing my health.

'Of course, I'm used to living in a warm climate and I know the precautions to take.' I was surprised at the defensive tone my thoughts took, as if I was bracing myself for a dressing down. 'This European sun's just as fierce as the Australian. I wear my cap everywhere and drink lots of water.'

'Good,' her voice came from somewhere. 'Don't forget your own advice. Remember your Cs and Ss. Meet all your challenges with courage, confidence and conviction and don't dash off seeking safe and secure answers.'

'Right, I'm not going to be beaten.'

'Very good,' she said.

CHAPTER 24

A crisis in confidence can be expected every now and then.
— From a card purchased at the bookshop in Brookings

I enjoyed chatting to students from other classes. I'd meet them on the way to school or walked with them as we returned to our residences. I met them on the streets, at the supermarket and at the superb Saturday markets. Some spoke English, but with many there was no common language other than French. I got to know one Japanese boy who regularly wore a Wallaby's guernsey. He had no English and not much French either, but we managed to communicate. There was a high turnover among the students. Some stayed for a week or two, others remained for months. You got used to the coming and going. You would meet and talk with someone, find out something of their background, establish a friendly, albeit ephemeral relationship, and then they disappeared.

The school's practice was to regrade the students each month. August not only brought cooler weather but also an assessment for all students. Everyone took a written examination; the new students did an oral test, the old lags took dictation.

'I enjoyed the written test but I'm worried about the dictation,' I said to Elaine when we met outside the school for a coffee after the exam. 'I've hated dictation since my school days. I'm reconciled to being demoted. They might have discovered I was a fraud being in the advanced class.'

'I'm sure you'll do alright,' Elaine reassured me. 'I'm hoping I'll do better. I'm hoping to move up to a higher class.'

'I'd be disappointed if I were dropped back, but, on the other hand, I would escape the torture. I've got to remind myself that I'm not doing this French caper for sheep stations.'

At the end of the day, the students gathered to see the results. We were given a glass of champagne, and then invited to study the results board. I found my name in the advanced list. Elaine found hers in the intermediate level. We had a celebratory drink at the Café Théâtre and a commiseration drink with Jack who was hoping for an upgrade.

Corinne had taken leave for the month and would be back in September. I found myself with new teachers. Our teachers for August were Michele and Pascaline. It would be fair to say Michele intrigued me. She was an older woman. She had an extensive wardrobe of tailored suits and wore a different outfit and accessories every day. She began with linen suits in the earlier warmer days but as the weather cooled over the month, the suits were heavier. She wore tweed on the last day. Her manner was formal (she always addressed me as 'Monsieur') and her teaching style was that of a lecturer. She was intrigued that I spoke to the other English speaking students in French even during the breaks.

Pascaline was tall, slim, young and beautiful. I would be lying if I did not admit she was very attractive. Many of the male students were in love with her. She also taught Jack's class. He told me he and his fellow male students regularly had her in their fantasies. I don't blame them.

I saw Elaine most days. I suggested we see a film one weekend. We arranged to meet at the Elephant Fountain and walked to the cinema. The film was *Le Principe d'Archimède*, a Spanish film with French sub-titles, a story of the ferocious rivalry between two women working together. One had to be very nimble indeed reading the sub-titles as the text appeared on the screen very briefly. The French speak quickly enough but the Spanish outrun them any day.

After the film I offered to walk Elaine home. As we neared her place, I made the comment that I hadn't walked a young girl home for many decades. I would have asked Elaine to dinner the same evening but another student Sophie, an English girl, was present when I mentioned the film. I felt embarrassed asking Elaine for a date. I hadn't asked a girl out for over forty-five years, that girl being Maris. The gossipy students would have had Elaine and me an item in no time.

During the week I told Elaine about Maris' shrine back in my apartment. She gave me a purple candle which was never her colour, but it came from Ireland, which was Maris' favourite destination. I asked Elaine to dinner the following Saturday.

I once questioned Philippe on the good restaurants of Chambéry and he had mentioned Le Grange. Elaine and I passed a very nice evening there. After a wine or two, she told me more of her story, particularly the impact of her divorce. She was a lost soul and grieving as much as I was. We had a

lot in common. We spoke a little in French but for the most
part conversed in English. One of the diners heard us and
asked me in French my country of origin. A big jovial fellow,
he announced that France and Australia would play the final
of the Rugby Union 2007 World Cup. He looked as if he
played rugby in his youth. I walked Elaine home and on the
way she reminded me of my comment after the film. I had
forgotten by then but I realised that she was very flattered. I
had won many Brownie points.

We had a very pleasant evening, enjoying each other's
company. As I walked back home through the park, passing
groups of young men having a drink, I felt that I had taken
several steps forward. I remembered the time the previous
November I went to the Sydney Jazz Club with Anne. I was
in tears as I drove to her place and felt a lack of fidelity to
Maris. This time I had no tears. Maris' name came up in
our conversation but I had no sense of disloyalty. I felt Maris
would have approved of my seeking out the company of an
agreeable lady. Something quite significant had happened.
I hoped I would see more of Elaine.

I was friendly with Anne and Ray. They were an American missionary couple. Anne was the missionary, Ray was
the pilot. Because the missionaries work in remote localities
they require light planes to get around. They had their three
children with them, Anneke, Peter and Andre. They had just
spent six years in Brazil where they spoke the local version of
Portuguese and their children went to a Portuguese school.
They were now in Chambéry learning French before taking
up their next appointment in the Cameroons. I marvelled at
the children — three intelligent youngsters who were being
reared in a variety of cultures. Anne was in my class and we

chatted every day. She invited me to dinner and I joined them one evening in their tiny apartment, not much larger in space than mine. It was fascinating to hear about the places they had been to in their missionary work.

They were interested in my writing so I gave them a copy of *Friend and Philosopher.* They asked me a lot of questions about Maris and her depression. Talking about Maris made me feel strongly for her, and as I walked back through the park on that night I had a minor wallop. I had to sit down on a park seat, among the young men having a drink, and recover before I returned to my apartment.

I realised I was still vulnerable. Grieving is hard work and has no timetable. It emerges in unexpected ways. It's like walking through a marsh. Most of the time you are walking on firm ground but every now and then you unexpectedly sink.

I was sad to see Anne and Ray depart on September 1st. They showed understanding and compassion, which would hold them in good stead in their missionary work.

I saw Jack regularly. He was busy planning his next record release and made a couple of trips to Brussels. We had our drinks after class and one night I invited him to dinner at my apartment. Later we met up with a number of other students. I found myself in a group at Le Cardinal, the student bar in the shadow of the cathedral. I continued to be amazed at the way these young people accepted me and invited me to join them. I was old enough to be their grandfather but they regarded me as one of them and I felt privileged to be accepted. It was their unexpected expressions of friendship which supported me the most, their words or gestures which transferred the energy of their good wishes. I could have been the old bloke, sitting alone in my apartment.

One morning I was walking through the park, having purchased an ethernet cable at a shop removed from the main centre. I did not take much notice of the old gentleman in front of me until just by the Palace de Justice he began staggering, clutched a post and fell to the ground. I ran to him, the first to arrive. He looked to me as if he was suffering a heart attack. I yelled out for help. A lady rang for the ambulance. Someone took his pulse. He was flat on his back gurgling. I helped turn him to the recovery position. We stood around for a few seconds. I thought I should try administering CPR and was about to start when a passer-by announced he was a doctor. He began the CPR but gained no response. In what seemed an incredible short time the ambulance arrived. They took over the CPR and used a Heartstart machine but the poor bloke didn't respond.

It was bizarre to see a fellow human die in front of you. Death is the last thing most of us have on our minds on a normal day, yet here I was witnessing an event which brought it to the forefront. I had to confront it. Death strikes at random. The last dead person I saw was Maris. I wondered if this old chap knew he was sick, if he had the chance to prepare for death. Did he have a family waiting for him to come home? I prayed for them.

That afternoon in class I mentioned my experience to my fellow students. Hussein, a doctor from Saudi Arabia, gave me some interesting statistics. He said that one in five recovers after receiving CPR. He also mentioned that Australia led the world in having the highest proportion of its population trained in CPR. I had a number of chats with Hussein. I respected him as an educated man but he had what I thought were ultra conservative attitudes towards women, a reflection of his culture, no doubt. A woman can only have sex with her husband. If his sister, for example, transgressed and had sex before or outside marriage, her act would bring great shame on the family. He would be forced to kill her or else kill himself. I still shudder at his attitude. (And I hope his sister behaves herself.)

* * *

Chambéry is surrounded by the Alps. I was keen to see something of the mountains, so one Sunday I seized the chance to join the school's excursion to the Parc National de la Vanoise, a national park on the border with Italy. The weather was perfect, a clear, cloudless and windless day. On the bus I met Mohamed, another Saudi Arabian doctor, Oke and Sardir, both Dutch university students, and Cosmo who was very English and spoke with a 'frightfully British' accent.

We drove through spectacular valleys to Pralagnon, situated at the edge of the park. The village was built for skiing. Chair lifts climbed the surrounding hills. We walked for ten kilometres up a steep incline to a level of 2500 metres, to a small lake at the foot of the glaciers. The others, many years my junior, ran up the slope like antelopes. I was determined to get there, too, so I persisted and arrived very much the last. The scenery was spectacular and I marvelled that I was at a height well above the highest mountain in Australia. On the steep walk down, I developed blisters on the ends of my toes. Cosmo entertained us with his mimicking innumerable accents, including Australian. Oke and Sardir mimicked various Dutch accents. I found it strange that in such a small country regional accents could have developed. I was stiff and blistered for several days. But overall my venture into the mountains was a valued experience.

I saw a lot of Cosmo during the two weeks he was at Chambéry. He, too, had an apartment in the Résidence Curial and we had dinner a number of times. He was keen to tell me his story. He attended the school the previous year during his holidays and had secretly fallen in love with the beautiful Pascaline. He managed to get into her classes again. He was a lost soul, too. He was adopted and had been seeking his origins. A reunion with his biological family was a disaster and he grieved for his lost roots. Rejection by his natural mother seemed to lie at the basis of his reasons for studying French and his interest in Pascaline, like a continuation of his adoption search. Poor fellow. He didn't have a good time at Chambéry and tormented himself with trying to get near Pascaline. He used to confide in me his manoeuvres. I wondered what Pascaline would have thought had she known.

A number of students departed at the end of the month, including Jack. I was sorry to see him leave. We had become good mates. I gave him a copy of *Friend and Philosopher* and he gave me one of his CDs. He was planning to return to San Francisco to undertake more recording, get himself a job and find some stability in his life.

Fortunately Elaine was staying another two weeks. One Sunday afternoon we saw an English film together. *The Wind that Stirs the Barley* was the English name but its title in French was *Le Vent Se Lève*. This time we had the benefit of English dialogue with French sub-titles. We had planned to dine at a restaurant but all were closed on Sunday evening, so I cooked dinner at my apartment.

Seeing Elaine as often as I did gave me a lot of satisfaction. I enjoyed her presence and I believed she enjoyed mine. But we had a definite time frame. We would be together for a limited time and then go our own ways like a holiday romance, except that we were interested in companionship rather than passion. I was very grateful to Elaine. I had taken a number of significant steps. She was teaching me what it was like to date a lady friend, to go out for an evening, enjoy her company and suffer no guilt or regret that I was being disloyal to Maris. It was like a practice run for when I returned. Many men who have been widowed would have been in another relationship by now — my good friend Paul for example. I was an eligible bachelor. Was I ready? I did not know. In other areas of adjustment to the loss of Maris, I had taken giant strides but in this relationships area, I was barely crawling.

CHAPTER 25

Dear Noel,
Our friendship has meant a lot to me during our time
here. Your conversation, warmth and your smile has kept
me going at times. Good luck with all the books that
come flowing through. Hope Lourdes goes better than
hoped and hopefully see you in Paris.
Take good care, have fun at all times and don't forget
to keep getting younger.
Elaine

I missed the AFL football. I had with me DVDs of the 2005 Finals, which Tim had given to me and I used to reward myself by playing a quarter at a time. I began to realise just how important the Sydney Swans were to me. As I cheered those young men, I thought of the many times I watched them with Maris. The Swans were more than a football team. They were far more than a diversion when there was nothing much on French TV. They were a link to the life we once shared. I thought of the many times we attended the Sydney Cricket Ground, eating sloppy meat pies and chips, and drinking a beer, rugged up against the cold, our pack backs full of wet weather gear, which we didn't mind donning provided the Swans won. Watching those DVDs became a ritual just as important as attending the games. Here I was in the south-east of France following the Swans. How many other passionately one-eyed Swans' supporters were following their team in remote corners of the globe? By season's end, they did their customary emotionally draining stuff of just winning or just losing but the good news was that they had made the final four.

September saw a further regrading of students. Once again all undertook a written examination. We old lags did dictation. Once again I was apprehensive about the dictation. Once again I was listed in the Advanced class. Most of August's class remained. We greeted each other warmly and welcomed the new students. We welcomed back a fired-up Corinne. I was positive and optimistic about September. Our first class with Corinne was stimulating.

My class mates were serious students. The 'tourists' had all gone back to their jobs or study. Hussein, the Saudi Arabian doctor, was hoping to study cardiology at Lyon Hospital. Marcus from Switzerland was studying four languages. He was interested in a career in diplomacy. Yolande, a Dutch girl, was planning to be a missionary in the Cameroons. Therese, an American, had married a Frenchman who had set up a Protestant church in Chambéry. Juan Carmello had left school in Columbia and wanted to study politics at a French university. Erkhardt was from Romania, Ruth from England, Sashiko from Japan, Maria from the Czech Republic, Ralph and Ursula from Germany. And here was I, a lost soul, studying 'pour le plaisir', humbled before these fluent speakers. Not to be daunted, I joined in class discussions and chatted haltingly in the breaks.

Corinne suggested that every student make a presentation on a topic of their choice. It was not obligatory but those who had the confidence should try. I didn't have the confidence but nevertheless I volunteered. I decided I would speak about my book *Friend and Philosopher* and present in French the same talk I had given to Rotary clubs. I stood nervously in front of the class. I spoke about the book's development, Maris' involvement, my activities in its promotion, the dedication to Maris and my decision to donate the profits to Lifeline. I explained the purpose of Lifeline. The inevitable question: what was the book about? I translated the back cover and read to the class. I explained that the purpose of the summary on the back cover was to hook the reader. Were they hooked? I asked. They said they were. I had ten copies left and I was prepared to give them to the English speakers or students of English. But no! They wanted to buy them so that the money could go to Lifeline. Their enthusiasm and generosity over-whelmed me. I set no price and when asked said, 'Comme vous voulez.' (Whatever you reckon). All together I received 130 euros. They were all convinced that one day I would be a famous author. Marcus invited me to speak to his English class back in Switzerland but I would have left Europe by the time his university was back at work.

I was pleased. Before I set out from Australia, I forwarded fifty copies of *Friend and Philosopher.* I was returning home with none. My books were scattered through America, England and Europe. A tiny, tiny beginning to a worldwide distribution?

The internet and the kid's emails kept me informed of the Sydney Swans' progress through the finals. They won by a point their first match against the West Coast Eagles.

They won against Fremantle which put them in the Grand Final, once again playing the West Coast Eagles, a repeat of the Grand Final of 2005. How I wished Maris was alive to witness these events. She had followed the Swans loyally in their time of struggle and now she was missing out on their stellar years.

I saw Elaine a few times before she departed. We had a last dinner at Chambéry's top restaurant, Le Bistrot, and over our Savoyard dinner we discussed our future plans. Before Chambéry Elaine had attended French classes in Bordeaux and was going on to Aix-en-Provence. After Aix-en-Province she was going back home to Ireland in time for Christmas. I was planning to join a pilgrimage to Lourdes, then travel through central France and spend the last ten days in Paris. I would concentrate on my writing in 2007. I would travel again one day. In the meantime I invited Elaine to join me in Paris on one of the two weekends I would be there should she want a break from Aix-en-Province. She seemed interested and said she put me in the small group of people she would like to keep in touch with. At our last lunch she slipped me a card.

* * *

In my last two weeks at Chambéry, I fell through a hole in the ice. For the first time in my trip I felt alone. My friends, Jack and Elaine, had departed. I became more conscious of the age difference to my fellow students. I had gained their respect rather than their friendship but I had no one to relax with over a drink. Jack, Elaine and I really did support each other in our struggle with the French language. We reminded each other that we were not playing for sheep stations. I lost confidence. Class became an effort, sometimes a torture. I began a countdown. Some classes went well, but in others I made so many errors I felt I had made no progress after almost three months. My written and grammar skills were good, but my oral skills...

My fellow students spoke with fluency and confidence but I muddled through. Corinne picked me up on my 'ums and ahhs' just as Maris did. Both Corinne and Nathalie commented on my pronunciation difficulties and lack of oral skills. A difficult dictation was particularly demoralising. Some days I was tempted to miss class, but being the masochist that I am, ever ready to confront difficult situations, I persevered, wondering why on earth I had put myself through all this effort.

At night, I missed Maris. It was so hard to believe she was not back in Australia waiting for me. My longing was intense. I sat before my shrine on top of the television — photos of Maris and I, the purple candle from Elaine, the little pot plant which had grown extra leaves and my driftwood cross. I talked to Maris and held the driftwood cross. I felt a spiritual presence and a connection with eternity. Alone in my narrow single bed, which was a settee by day and has to be made up each evening, I thought of Maris and fantasised making love to her. Afterwards she would cuddle up to me and as she slept she would chase me through the night for the warmth from my body. We found fulfilment and deep satisfaction in our sex life, a wonderful way of expressing our love, providing a privateness that excluded all others. Love is the deepest part of the human heart and touches profound depths within us. Without love, our lives are in danger of withering and dying.

Under the influence of a strong cocktail of grief and desire, I was engaged in an internal battle with no chance of winning. Sex, like a smouldering fire, flared up, occupying both body and mind, strong, dominating and impatient. I wanted to masturbate. I tried to get some meaning from these urges. Masturbation was not just wanking, but a celebration of the sexual life I once had with Maris. I had taken several backward steps to a time after Maris' death when my longing for sexual contact with her overwhelmed me. I'm a sexual being, God made me that way. I wanted to make love to Maris but to no one else. I was not interested in prostitutes or one night stands. In Chambéry I passed a sex shop and a brothel every day on the way to the school but I had no intention of making inquiries.

Sex should be part of a committed relationship, not for casual acquaintances, certainly not for a leisure pastime like playing tennis. The French may not have understood my scruples; they have a delightfully relaxed attitude towards sex, including masturbation. Only harmful if the person feels guilty, too normal an activity to get worried about. The questions churned around my brain. Like all human beings, I have a spiritual, sensual and sexual side. The calm times are when all three are integrated and seem to be in balance. The rough times are when the three go to war with each other. Throw in my Catholic upbringing and I was in troubled waters. I wonder how many men of my generation, good blokes, don't have some sexual damage because of a deeply ingrained, unnecessary sense of guilt. Many, no doubt, have learned to ignore it, but it is there, nevertheless, lurking in the background, doing its damage.

The torments continued to plague me. After forty-two

years of a successful and happy marriage, in which we both offered ourselves to each other fully and without reservation, could I develop a relationship with another woman, a relationship which could lead beyond companionship to a more intimate phase involving commitment and love? This was the question. I have my needs for companionship and intimacy. I cannot deny or suppress my sexual interests. They are part of the human condition. They must dominate the mind and body of every male. On the other hand, I did not want to develop a relationship just for the sex. These are issues which must face every widow and widower.

There was no protection from these vexations. The hour before dawn was the worst and, as I faced the day, I had to remember to meet my challenges with Cs rather than Ss.

Tortured by day and tormented by night I was looking forward to leaving Chambéry and moving to the next stage of my trip. All arrangements for the pilgrimage to Lourdes were in place. I was to finish my course on Friday 29th September and depart for Lourdes the following Tuesday. The pilgrimage might offer me relief from my spiritual confusion, an opportunity to blend the spiritual and sensual elements of my being, to rediscover and develop new confidence. I needed to develop aspirations and choose means to live them.

Tim rang. He had managed to get two tickets for the Grand Final. He offered Angela the other ticket which she accepted with enthusiasm, dropping everything to fly down to Melbourne.

Back in class I developed a friendship with nineteen year old Juan Carmello. I noticed considerable growth in the two months that I knew him. At first his black hair was bubbly and he looked a child. He had his hair cut and overnight he seemed to mature and become a young man. He had been reared by his grandparents back in Columbia and come to France after leaving school hoping to study at a French university. He was highly motivated, excellent with his French and by far the best student. He was in the process of applying to universities. It was a quaint friendship considering the age difference. Yet we were equals, both with our goals and aspirations. I wished him well with his studies and career and he wished me well with my writing.

My last days in class arrived quickly. I said goodbye to my fellow students and gave Corinne my pot plant. She was touched. A graduation ceremony was held at the end of every month at which the departing students were given a certificate from the Institut Français de Chambéry. Now it was my turn. The ceremony was held at the Château du Ducs de Savoie. All the teachers were present. Over champagne, the certificates were handed out by the president of the Academie de Savoie, an old chap who looked to be in his nineties. I was pleased with my certificate. I received the highest award, 'Félicitations des Professeurs' (Congratulations from the teachers), Excellent and Très Bon (very good) in every category except Oral Expression. I knew oral expression would be my weakness.

As we left the Chateau I walked with a group of Japanese students, including the boy with the Wallaby guernsey. He delighted in showing the word Australia printed on the back. I always got on well with the Japanese. I was always interested in Japan from a child. I remember during the war years the propaganda cartoons which depicted Japanese children with buck teeth being trained to bayonet the Aussie soldiers. As a ten year old I used to think they couldn't be that bad. They're kids just like us. Maris and I spent a month in Japan in the early eighties, our first overseas trip together. We found the Japanese gracious and incredibly polite. I told these students that I had actually visited their country and some of their native towns. None of the European students had been to Japan. They invited me to have dinner with them on my last night as a student. What a group! Six young Japanese and a seventy-three year old Australian conversing in broken French! They were enthusiastic yet gracious and incredibly polite.

On Saturday morning I was woken at 6 am by a text message from Angela. She and Tim were at the Melbourne Cricket Ground for the AFL Grand Final. The game was about to start. I turned on my laptop and followed the match via a diagram representing the passage of play. Angela sent texts with the score at quarter time and half time. The Swans were well behind, not unusual for them. It was still dark at Chambéry so I stayed in bed and I went back to sleep. I was woken at three quarter time with a text from Angela. The Swans had made their come back and I had missed it. I switched to one of the radio stations and listened to the last quarter. The Swans lost by a point.

I found myself rebuking Maris. 'You should have used your influence,' I said as I showered to get ready for the day.

'The Swans had their turn last year.' I seemed to hear her voice in the sound of the running water. 'It's fair that some-one else should win the Grand Final this year.'

What had I learned in my three months at Chambéry? Chambéry lies in a beautiful part of France. It was once the capital of Savoy, so it is drenched in history and natural beauty. I enjoyed its summer festivals, full of colour and pageantry, and the many excursions I made into the surrounding towns and countryside. I met some great people, all of whom had their influence on my emotional and spiritual travelling. I'm sure my French is better. I developed confidence and was less likely to allow fluent speakers to intimidate me. But I hadn't come up with any answers to the questions plaguing me. Since Maris' death I had experienced an inner restlessness, an emptiness which longed to be filled. I'm not sure whether my inner desire was a longing to have Maris back, or whether I was searching for another reality.

Maybe I would find an answer in Lourdes.

Chapter 26

Pilgrimages have been popular through the ages and among all people because the outer journey becomes a symbol to the pilgrim for the meaning of life, expressing in a physical gesture a deep interior longing of the soul to reach its final destination.
— Harvest Pilgrimages website, 2009

Catholics have been undertaking pilgrimages to Lourdes since 1872, just a few years after the apparitions of the Blessed Virgin to a young peasant girl, Bernadette. Nowadays, about three million people visit Lourdes each year. Some go as individuals, some in groups. My pilgrimage to Lourdes was the Pèlerinage du Rosarie (pilgrimage of the rosary), organised by the Dominicans since 1907 and held first week of October. The theme for 2006 was Lumière du Christ (light of the Christ) — passing from the darkness into the light. As I had been without much light for the last two years, these four days could be an opportunity to renew my spiritual resources.

Tuesday morning saw me leaving Chambéry at 7.30 on the crowded commuter train for Grenoble where I joined a special pilgrimage TGV. We stopped at towns along the way to pick up more pilgrims and soon the train was full. I later learned that six other TGVs were departing from other parts of France and that about 40,000 pilgrims would be attending.

I was anxious, close on terror, probably the only non-French person (let alone Australian) on a train packed with French people speaking their regional accents. Would my stilted French, developed in the artificial atmosphere of the language school, be up to it? It would be an understatement to say I was feeling well out of my comfort zone.

'If I'm so keen to visit Lourdes,' I found myself asking Maris, 'why didn't I join an English-speaking group?'

As things turned out, I had absolutely nothing to worry about. The people were welcoming, enthusiastic and excited. It wasn't long before everyone was talking to each other and I found myself involved in the chatter. What a contrast to the language school. Here I was one of the younger pilgrims. Many women were wearing uniforms. Hostesses wore blue, nurses wore white. There were many sick people aboard. We were given a beautifully produced booklet containing the prayers, chants, scripture reading, and details of all the ceremonies and the various meetings and services. The language was simple and poetic, easy to read. We were each given a scarf. Each of the regions had their own colour. Ours was pink.

A priest lead the rosary through the PA system — the first time I'd said the rosary for years. Very popular in my childhood, it had fallen out of fashion among today's Australian Catholics. I'd forgotten the names of the mysteries but I was prepared. I had bought a pair of beads in Chambéry. We said the rosary a number of times. It reminded me of my childhood and my early days with Maris when we used to say the rosary going on a trip. I was going back to the basics of our Catholic practices.

The journey lasted fourteen hours. We travelled half way across France, passing through many well known cities — Nimes, Montpellier, Narbonne, Carcassonne, Toulouse. I was not a tourist today. I had my pilgrim hat on and was more interested in what was going on inside the train, getting to know my fellow passengers, my fellow pilgrims travelling on the road together. All were interested in my situation as I was the odd one out. When I told Maggie I had never been to Lourdes, she gave me an article outlining its history. I had written out the Our Father and the Hail Mary in French. I checked with her that my translation was correct. 'Parfait!' she assured me.

Opposite me sat Gabriel and his wife Geneviève together with her mother, whose name I never knew. She was a very chirpy old lady full of anticipation for her pilgrimage. All three of them had been to Lourdes several times. Geneviève was a retired French teacher. She was very interested in my efforts to learn the language. We conversed for hours on a wide range of subjects — rearing families, the degeneration of the young of today and their indifference to the beauties of the French language, whether one had to believe in the apparitions at Lourdes. She was liberal in outlook and had much the same attitude as I did to some of the authoritarian attitudes of the Catholic Church. She was very good to me, the teacher in her correcting my grammar and pronunciation. She taught me as much as Corinne.

At first I thought Giles and Gabriel (another Gabriel) were father and son, but actually Giles, the younger man, was

Gabriel's carer. Giles had been on this pilgrimage twelve times and Gabriel ten. I found their accent difficult to understand, as if they were speaking another language. Geneviève's mother flirted with old Gabriel. When he wouldn't share his lunch with her, she accused him of lacking Christian charity.

A tired group of pilgrims arrived at 9.30 pm. From the railway station we were taken by buses to our hotels. Mine was the Sainte Rose. We were given a late meal and I met the two couples who would be my dinner companions. That night, I reflected as I discussed the day with Maris. It did not matter if I did not totally believe in the apparitions. What mattered was that I should put my scepticism aside and be totally open to the experience, sharing the next four days with thousands of others. I was prepared to allow time and space to collapse around me. Instead of being the detached observer, I would throw myself into this pilgrim business.

My meal companions were Pierre and Gabrielle and Lucien and Edmonda, all from Grenoble. Enthusiastic pilgrims, they had been to Lourdes many times. Pierre was sick and used a wheelchair. He was quite a character. He talked so much that Gabrielle had to remind him to eat. Lucien was quiet but Edmonda made up for him. The banter between the couples saddened me. It reinforced I was on my own. I thought of the banter that Maris and I pursued. Between them, the four knew about six words of English. They spoke at 200 kilometres a minute but they were generous and included me, making sure that, by getting the gist of the conversation, I could contribute. We also had some discussions about whether you had to believe in the apparitions or not. My contribution was that it didn't matter whether you believed in them or not. The main thing to believe in was hope, which I think is what Lourdes is all about.

Then followed four days of ceremonies. Several times I visited the grotto where the apparitions of Our Lady occurred. I felt a definite presence. I joined the queue to file around the back of the grotto, touched the rock face and noted the spring, said to have flowed after one of the apparitions. The faith and devotion of the people was striking, many just standing around with their rosary beads, others kneeling on the wet ground in the rain. Many of the sick wait there, hoping for a miracle and a cure. Each evening at 9 pm, wet or fine, a procession of the Light began. Thousands walked with candles, singing songs and chants and saying the rosary, waving the candles each time *Ave Maria* was sung. (We waved our scarfs in daylight.)

My pilgrimage to Lourdes reminded me of earlier days and the way we expressed our faith. Catholic devotions centred on Mary, the Rosary and Stations of the Cross. I was back in time, not in a negative sense, but with the basics of my faith, similar to the way that a football coach might speak to a team about getting back to basics if they wanted to win the game.

Being a pilgrim was hard work. God gave me a sensual side as well as a spiritual one and, by the time I had attended Mass, did the Stations of the Cross three times, walked up the steep hill, said many rosaries, joined a procession of the sick in the afternoon and the procession of the light at night, I was in need of a beer back at the Sainte Rose hotel.

In addition to the ceremonies, there were many other activities, some for adolescents and young adults, some for the divorced and remarried, even for rural Christians. The group that attracted my attention was a Catholic movement called *Espérance et Vie* (Hope and Life), which supports widows and widowers in the early years. I know of no similar movement in Australia. I was keen to know more. They ran group information sessions which I attended. *Espérance et Vie* is a national organisation with head office in Paris and branches in all the French dioceses and in other French speaking countries. They hold regular meetings and conferences. They publish books and pamphlets which are extracts from talks given at their various conferences. I bought three — *Suicide*, *A New Marriage* and *Sexuality among the Bereaved*. I also bought one of their books –*Traverser le Veuvage* (Getting through Widowhood). Back at the Saint Rose hotel I read those pamphlets late into the night. Those issues related to new relationships and sexuality, all of which were discussed in typical French fashion so frankly.

The next day I had a session with one of the *Espérance et Vie* counsellors. She had herself been widowed for eighteen years and raised challenging questions about whether I was ready to leave the past behind me, to accept that life with Maris had been accomplished, that I had freedom to move on.

'Are you still clinging to a past that can never be repeated?' would be a rough translation of the question she posed. She drew on her own experience of the struggles she had during her early years of widowhood and described her present serenity even though she had not formed a new relationship. I was pleased that my grasp of French was sufficient to discuss my concerns. The discussion helped clear my mind and to look at where I was at and where I could be.

The pilgrimage concluded Saturday lunch so Saturday

afternoon was the only time I had to look around the town. With three million visitors a year it's not surprising that it's full of hotels and souvenir shops, the sanctuary itself free of commercial activity. As gifts for friends and family I bought a number of candles with the message 'This light prolongs my prayer'.

Back on the train Sunday morning I found myself seated with the same people. Everyone was excited and enthusiastic, all talking at once, keen to relate their experiences and asking me for my impressions. I had loaded my photos on to my laptop and the people wanted to see not only my photos of Lourdes but my other photos of France. So I put on a slide show. As we chatted, exchanging our experiences, people told me some of their stories. Maggie's husband was a petrol tanker driver. An accident left him seriously burned. Maggie nursed him for ten years until his death the year before. Life was lonely for her. Geneviève was worried about her mother. I had noticed her mother, in contrast to the earlier trip, was very quiet. She seemed exhausted as if the pilgrimage had worn her out. The older Gabriel was philosophical about whether death would catch up with him before he got to another pilgrimage. Giles worked on the railways. He wasn't too happy about going back to the job. I was very gratified to receive an invitation from Gabriel and Geneviève to visit them in their village. I felt as one with these pilgrims.

I had an extraordinary experience. I met people, not the ones the average tourist would contact in hotels or restaurants, but ordinary everyday folk. People are the same everywhere. Once you try to talk to them in their language and reach out to them, they accept and trust you, they want to talk about their families and the major burdens of their lives. In turn they want to know about your family and your life. Maris would have loved to hear their stories, too. Had she known French, she, too, would have found these conversations the most stimulating part of her journey.

I was sad to leave my pilgrim friends. I could understand why so many have gone on pilgrimages so often. One day I will go on another.

CHAPTER 27

This light prolongs my prayer.

I said goodbye to my fellow pilgrims at Grenoble and took the train back to Chambéry. As I walked back to my apartment, I entered a kebab shop to buy milk. 'C'est Noël,' I heard. There were Juan Carmello and the Japanese boy in his Wallaby guernsey, buying their dinner. Juan Carmello was keen to hear about Lourdes. He told the news at the school and the new students. Corinne was his teacher. Once again, we wished each other well.

I gave myself two more days at Chambéry to pack and extract myself emotionally. I visited the cathedral on Monday and lit a candle for Maris. I visited the cathedral again on Tuesday for the last time. Maris' candle was still burning. I had not visited any of the museums in Chambéry. I tried to remedy this omission only to find that museums are closed on Tuesday so I walked up the hill behind my apartment and sat in the garden of J J Rousseau, among the apple trees some of which Rousseau himself planted, peacefully admiring for the last time the beautiful view over this ancient town.

I spent the last ten days of my trip in Paris in an apartment in Les Halles. I established a shrine for Maris with my cross, a candle and her photo. As I meditated in front of her temporary shrine, I thought of how she would have enjoyed these days in Paris. I thought of her sisters, Catherine and Loretta.

'What a different world I would be living in, Maris, if the three of you had been growing old together, swapping recipes, sharing stories about the families, advising each other on your problems, and doing all the little things that sisters do together.'

I settled quickly into the tourist routine, walked extensively and made full use of the metro. I returned to the 5th Arrondisement where I stayed last time in Rue des Parmes and went around the corner to one of my favourite churches, St Etienne du Mont. I visited all the usual tourist sites, getting the impression that there are more tourists than Parisians in Paris. I can appreciate Paris' reputation as one of the most visited cities in the world.

I received an email from Elaine. She told me of her experiences at Aix-en-Provence but made no mention of visiting Paris. I was disappointed. I would have enjoyed her companionship sightseeing together.

My visit to Grace Cathedral was a practice run for a new spiritual experience. Chartres was an hour's train ride from Gare Montparnasse. The only difficulty was the walk from the Montparnasse metro to the Grand Ligne station. All underground, it goes up and down stairs and escalators, along a walkway travelling at nine kilometres per hour (amazing to see so many motionless people being whisked at such a speed), with innumerable sidetracks. It truly is a maze but there are sufficient signposts not to lose your way.

At Chartres the cathedral was very easy to find as it

dominates the town. The building is breathtaking. If you visit as a tourist you will find an outstanding model of aesthetic achievement, but, if you visit as a pilgrim, you will enter a wonderful instrument of religious action, of a faith expressed in stone that generates its own energy. If you give yourself the time to appreciate the beauty, to absorb its harmony, and not rush on to the next tourist thing, it's difficult not to be inspired. I admired the magnificent stained glass windows and the carvings, but was disappointed to find the labyrinth covered with chairs. It was impossible to view, let alone to walk. I inquired at the cathedral's bookshop, 'Is the labyrinth ever uncovered?'

'Yes, on Fridays,' the sales person said.

The day was Wednesday, so Friday saw me on the train again.

The labyrinth was installed between 1194 and 1220. Its single path design represents the journey of the spirit. It's a path of prayer and reflection, walked for spiritual insight and healing. It's not a maze. A maze is designed to lose your way. A labyrinth is designed for you to find your way. It's a metaphor for our own spiritual journey.

This time all the chairs had been placed to one side to reveal its full extent. The path is clearly defined and the stones are very smooth from millions of feet. I was taken aback by this first sighting. I had thought about this moment since visiting Grace Cathedral. I had come a long way to see it. I felt that love and wisdom were somehow mixed up with my experience in a way I couldn't explain. People of faith had been walking the path for generations and I was about to join a brotherhood. I felt small and humble, and heard the prayers of pilgrims long gone to God.

For a time, I sat and observed. There was a steady stream of visitors, nothing like the crowds at Notre Dame de Paris. Some had their heads in the air admiring the beautiful stained glass windows and didn't notice what was under their feet. Others looked with amusement at the bare-footed people already on the labyrinth. Some treated it as a game and dashed quickly with their friends along its path, as if impatient to fit in the next tourist thing.

I walked the labyrinth twice, the second time in bare feet on a cold, gritty floor. Both times I held the driftwood cross. I found the combination of the cross and the labyrinth powerful. Both are timeless in their own way. To me the labyrinth represented my journey up to the moment, the turns the significant mileposts in my life. The path of the labyrinth is clearly defined. I could see where I'd been. The sense of being open to what lies ahead came clearly to me as I left the labyrinth. There's no clearly defined path to follow at the exit. You really have to leave the past behind and be ready to go where God leads. Where that was, I hadn't a clue.

Uppermost in my mind was Maris and the input I received from Espérance et Vie at Lourdes. Was I ready to leave the past behind me, to accept that my life with Maris was accomplished, that I had the freedom to move on, to be open to what lay ahead, perhaps to seek a new relationship, while still treasuring Maris' memory and our life together? Was I prepared to say to myself, 'I am alone, having had the experience of being one of a couple with Maris. Am I ready to consider being one of another couple which will be very different but will give me the opportunity for the intimacy which I have missed so much?'

A few months previously I would have dismissed such

questions as disloyalty, but now, as I reflected in this magnificent cathedral, feeling close to reality and still under the spell of the labyrinth, I wanted to liberate myself from restraints, let go of the brakes, as it were, and give myself permission to seek another life. I would continue to grieve for Maris, probably that would never stop, but perhaps I could integrate my grief into a new life and relationship.

CHAPTER 28

Let the wind from the good old sea blow in to bathe the
wound and let it sting.
— Michael Leunig

The plane came into Sydney from the west. It was early morning but the sun had already risen and cast its light over the landscape. The harbour and bays passed under our view. Water shone like ribbons of light from the dark earth. The plane kept going eastwards over the coast then back steeply and turned back to the airport. Full of anticipation, I looked out the window straight down to the ocean and the coast racing to meet us. The plane straightened and dropped towards the ground. A slight bump and I was back in Australia. The collective sigh suggested that I was not the only passenger glad to be home.

Badly in need of sleep, I went through immigration and customs almost on automatic and walked out to the waiting crowd. Almost immediately I spotted Angela and Jacinta, both of them vigorously waving. It was wonderful to see their familiar faces and the grandchildren's as well, full of smiles and welcome, probably thoroughly briefed by their parents not to ask Pa if he had bought any presents for them. Thank God for my family: my children and my grandchildren. Even though I was on the other side of the world, they reached out to me through their emails, text messages and phone calls. They were there all the time. Without their support, I may not have coped. My heart aches for those who have to face catastrophe without family or supportive network.

As I walked out of the airport, I knew my supportive community was waiting. Where would I be without the love of my family, my fellow parishioners at St Anthony's, my family group, my friends at Lifeline, the Catenians? If I did not have my networks, if I had to face the loss of Maris alone, how could I survive? Maris' suicide has revealed to me the rich colours of kindness and generosity, the importance of friendship.

The first thing I noticed at home was Maris' tree. In the five months I was away, it had flourished and added a few metres. It was tall, slim and elegant, just like Maris. It was looking more and more like its neighbour, the peppermint gum, which dominates the back yard. Two such trees would be too much. I knew I should be practical and remove it before it got too large, but, with a flash of insight, I realised that the tree was sign of my belief in a tomorrow.

I had arranged my timing to be home with the family for the second anniversary of Maris' death. I had planned nothing. The next day, weary from the long flight and jet lag, I walked to the cemetery and visited Maris. I was glad to be back with her. I sat quietly on the familiar seat near her grave and said G'day. It seemed a long time since I last visited, but it also seemed a few days. The same wind gently stirred the bushes and shrubs, the same air was peaceful, the same birds twittered in the trees, the same cockatoos made their racket, the same Australian sun shone fiercely.

Two days later, on her anniversary, I visited Maris with the family. The grandchildren ran among the graves. Two rows down from Maris, on the grave of a young child, was a line of toy cars. The children made straight for them and played with them. Angela and Jacinta had to keep track of the toys and ensure they were back in their place when we left. After two years of visiting the cemetery I am surprised those toys are still there. One could chastise the grandchildren for being disrespectful, but their exuberance reflects their pleasure in the moment, their joy for life.

I was content to be back with Maris at home. I had sensed her presence at Chambéry, I often found myself in mental conversation with her. I felt her spirit on the beach in Oregon. She travelled with me on aeroplanes and trains. Her presence was not physical; rather, it nestled deep in my heart and spoke to me from within. Back home, there was so much real evidence of her having lived in this house. Her clothes in the wardrobe, her notebooks on the bookshelf, her handwriting in our address book, and her three shrines. Her camera, still loaded with the film she shot of the family the night before she died, lay in the cupboard.

I was back home in my world. My time in France was a memory. It was as if during my time at Chambéry, Lourdes and Chartres I was contained in a room and I was under the illusion that the reflection in the windows was the real world and there was nothing outside. Now back in Frenchs Forest, on the northern beaches of Sydney, I had left that illusion behind and, no doubt about it, here I was in my real world.

I ran my hands over Maris' clothes. I felt close to her

and imagined her wearing them. Here was the outfit she bought for Angela's wedding, here were her slacks, here was a blue cocktail dress that I always admired. She always looked elegant in them; they suited her tall, slim figure. I sat on our familiar bed where we had shared so many nights cuddled together. I found myself reflecting as I did in Chartres Cathedral just a few days previously. What did I receive from Espérance et Vie at Lourdes? Was I ready to leave the past behind me? Was I ready to accept that my life with Maris was accomplished, that I had the freedom to move on, to be open to what lay ahead, perhaps to seek a new relationship, while still treasuring Maris' memory and our life together? Back in Chartres Cathedral, I experienced a sense of freedom as if I was liberating myself from restraints, but here at home, surrounded by Maris' presence, my reaction was quite different. I may be open to the future, but I was definitely not ready to leave the life I lived with Maris behind. I did not want to be liberated. I wanted to be held by the golden chains of Maris' memory. Perhaps later I could let go of the brakes and give myself permission to progress to another life, continuing to grieve for Maris, but integrating my grief into a new life and relationship, but not yet. I had done some healing but I wasn't ready to close the chapter.

I looked around our bedroom and thought of our life together. Evidence of it was everywhere, in her clothes, in the bedding, in the bed itself, in my wedding ring which I continue to wear. I had lost Maris but I'll never lose the years with her, from the evening I first met her at the Heidelberg Town Hall to the morning of her death. Even though she's gone, she's still part of my life and the family's. I reminded myself I should think more of her sixty six years of life and the forty-two years we had together, and not dwell compulsively on the one moment of death. I had been blaming myself so often, but I should think about all those years I supported her and not about the apparent one moment of neglect. In the early days of my grieving I thought I could never forgive myself, but now, two years later, I was well on the way.

I added the purple candle which Elaine had given me to the shrine in the family room and placed one of the candles I bought at Lourdes before the shrine in the bedroom.

I was not ready to sit around and mope, to use one of Maris' phrases. I drew on Maris' spirit and soon moved back into life. I caught up with family news. At my first appearance at St Anthony's, I was welcomed back. I attended the Catenian's meeting. President Garry was enthusiastic in his welcome. I contacted the Lifeline office and organised some shifts. I felt I was ready to dispose of some of Maris' clothing, so each time I visited Lifeline I took some for the opportunity shops. I retained a few garments which I liked or had special significance, like the dresses she wore to the kid's weddings. They occupied a small amount of hanging space, ready for me to look at or handle whenever I wished.

I wondered about my literary grant application. I had no calls so I assumed I was unsuccessful. I did not expect a grant, but I was determined to write on my journey, whether or not I had the support of the Australia Council, because I believed I had something to share. I wanted to tell the world how I handled my loss. In the midst of my darkness, I found the sun within myself. If it can prevent some damage by helping others survive their bereavement, if the many families who have suffered from the pain and anguish of the suicide of a loved one gain some strength from sharing my experience, my story will have done its work. My hope is that my journey will be recognised as authentic by others who have suffered a similar loss. I hoped, too, that the general reader might gain an appreciation of the huge task facing the bereaved.

I would also be writing for myself. I was facing a lifelong sorrow and one way of reducing its burden is by using the experience to offer relief to others travelling similar paths. Healing energy had already come my way. Bit by bit the broken pieces were being put together. The wound was healing over, but now I was prepared to uncover it and let it lie open. I knew it would be hard to make what James back at the Winchester Writers' Conference called a misery memoir sound engaging, but I was going to have a go. I needed to tell my story.

And press on I did in writing this book. I had my research to do. I looked over what I had submitted to the Australia Council. I spent time reading the many tribute letters. As I read, I was amazed how many lives Maris had touched and actually helped to make a difference. I browsed through the notebooks Maris had left behind. They were her journals, part of her efforts to gain insight into the illness that was inflicting so much suffering on her. I consulted my journal. I had kept a journal since Maris died. Writing the journal was a therapy in itself. It allowed me to record my fears and insights, to think more clearly and that in turn helped to develop strategies. I had gained some wisdom about the process of grieving.

I set myself the goal of writing every day. It became a task which I looked forward to. I had set myself a significant challenge. As I reread my submission to the Australia Council, I met head on the harrowing details of the first few days. I was saddened but my feelings were not as intense. Time had softened my sorrow but the memory will never vanish in the mists. Maris' suicide had trampled on every aspect of my being. Nothing escaped — my whole way of life, my energy, my spirit, my body, feelings, emotions, pleasures, sense of fun, will, my attitudes to others, and those private things which I would normally have kept to myself.

By that time I had done enough work on *Whistler Street* so I sent the manuscript to the publisher for comment. The reaction was favourable. The manuscript was worthy of publishing although the reviewer didn't like the ending. Neither did I, so I set about rewriting it before sending the manuscript back to go through the editing and design process.

I discovered that one of my neighbours, Frank, had died while I was overseas. Frank and his wife Edna had lived in the neighbourhood well before Maris and I arrived. I used to have chats with Frank. He was a heart attack waiting to happen, he'd told me.

Frank's death confirmed what I had been thinking since Maris died. Life is by no means reliable. Nothing can be taken for granted and nothing can be presumed. Everything has to grow, breathe and perish in its own way, its own place and time. We all have expectations and it can take a lifetime to have acceptance without expectation. You have to let go. I felt that Frank had accepted his precarious situation. He was not fussed about his impending death. I spoke to Edna to offer my condolences. She said she missed Frank.

I received a letter from Anne. Was I interested in going to the Sydney Jazz Club annual ball again? Last year I shed a tear as I drove to her house but this year I was relaxed as we drove to the Drummoyne RSL Club. The same people were at the table. The same band, the Café Society orchestra led by Geoffrey Ogden Brown, played similar music — My Dog Bradman, When you're in love, Pennies in Heaven, Drummer Boy, Pasadena, Black Bottom Stump, Lucky Lindy, Hilton Stomp, Trombone Rag, Gigolo, an Al Jolson medley. The crowd was dressed in feathers and black. Again the scene was a time warp from the twenties. Anne and I danced most of the evening. The same septuagenarians and octogenarians from last year were dancing, too. The evening was fun. I had none of the regrets from last year of being disloyal to Maris. I had moved on a little. I had put some of the pieces back.

* * *

The end of November saw a Bereavement Mass one warm, balmy, cloudless evening at St Anthony's. There was Maris' name along on the list. Everyone placed a carnation on the altar as the name of their loved one was read. My eyes were dry. I was saddened but my feelings were by no means as ferocious as on previous occasions. The liturgy was adequate, I suppose, but an ideal opportunity was missed when outside the cicadas stirred. I did not hear noisy insects disturbing the flow of the service. I heard in their song the spirits of all our departed love ones responding to our prayers. Their song rather than the service inspired me and gave me the resolve to press on.

I flew to Brisbane for a quick visit to my sister Maria. Maria and Joe were well. No illnesses or operation during my absence this time. I told Maria my plans, that I would concentrate on promoting *Whistler Street* as soon as it was published and begin writing the account of my journey.

She echoed Maris when she said, 'You don't sit around and mope.'

On the Sunday afternoon their retirement village had a dance. There were plenty of dancers. I was conscious of being without a partner. One of the village residents, Peter, asked a few questions about my story. I was perhaps more open than I needed to be as I sensed I did not have an insightful companion.

'You ought to be moving on,' he said. 'Don't hesitate to search for a new wife.'

I was taken aback by his comments, given that he really knew nothing about me, apart from being Maria's brother. It would be fair to say I was staggered at my reaction, how his unsolicited advice upset me. It made me realise just how vulnerable I still was. At an earlier stage, his limited understanding would have almost defeated me. He didn't appreciate that healing takes its own time and travels at a different pace in each person. He was telling me what he would have done. If he had lost a wife, he would have promptly found a replacement. I found the idea repulsive.

There were a number of ladies on their own, widows I think. I should have done the right thing and asked one or two to dance, but I could not mask my feelings. Peter's attitude brought on a reticence and I could not force a smile and a gallant attitude while my spirit hurt. While the music and the dancing whirled about me, I mulled over the question. Was I ready to leave Maris behind and go hunting for a new mate?

It's clear to me that to remarry solely for the purpose of not being a widower and not being alone is not sufficient reason. If I were to marry a second time, it would be to build a new relationship, to have a new companion on the road and not to overcome difficulties in being a widower. The loneliness is a burden, for sure. It would be good to love and be loved anew, to have someone to share the joys and sorrows, the travelling, exchanges of view. But not at any price.

I made myself fully known to Maris. I placed my complete trust in her. My love for Maris is too strong. Her presence lives within me. We had forty-two years together. She was a wonderful person. I realise you idealise a person after their death, but that does not detract from her generous and compassionate nature. Am I capable of loving another? Would I trust another person as completely? Would I make myself fully known? Would I find another person with the same admirable qualities? Would anyone else measure up to her? Would I find myself always comparing other 'eligible' ladies to Maris?

We built up our love and relationship over many years. We reared our family together. We faced our joys and sorrows as one with common values and priorities in life. We lived our whole lives together and succeeded in finding a balance. Would I find another woman with whom I could establish this equilibrium? Would I be able to make concessions? Would I be sufficiently malleable? Would I succeed in developing complete and total trust and confidence in another woman?

Would a second wife be able to live with a husband who had buried the love and memories of his first wife deep in his heart, who has filled his house with her memories, whose presence dwells in every room? Would this second wife want to live with a man who seeks to perpetuate his former wife's memory through the sales of his books? All have been dedicated to her. Her photograph is at the front. Every time a reader opens the book they will see her photo and read the dedication.

I have made progress in many areas. But in this relationship area, I have hardly moved. I have not even begun to seek out other ladies just for their companionship. Elaine has been the only lady whom I have dated. As lost soul students in Chambéry, we were thrown together and sought each other for companionship. She taught me to believe that being with another lady was okay. When I left France and returned to Australia I thought I might be ready to seek other women for steady companionship, but as soon as I was back in my home and felt the presence of Maris, I knew I had a long way to go. One of these days. Perhaps.

Twenty Nine

I have a plan for you; a plan not to harm you but to give you hope for the future.
— Jeremiah 29:11

Early one Thursday morning I experienced chest pains. I had such pain previously from time to time, particularly when under some stress, but didn't take much notice as they went away after a short time. I mentioned them to Jacinta who insisted I see my doctor so I made an appointment for that morning. The doctor quizzed me on my lifestyle. I attended a gym three times a week. I walked the other days. My food intake was balanced. My height and weight were normal. He took my blood pressure which was normal. He did a blood test. Cholesterol was normal. Everything seemed normal. 'Is there a history of heart problems in the family?' he asked.

'My mother died of a heart attack.'

He did an ECG. The results were irregular, the message on the screen indicating an earlier infarction. He said I should see a cardiologist. I rang and an appointment was made for the following Tuesday for a stress test. The results were similarly irregular and the message was the same. The cardiologist wanted me to have an angiogram. There was a degree of urgency, he said, and booked me in for the Thursday.

I was bemused. Everything was happening so quickly. I had my consultation with my GP the previous Thursday, and here I was, a week later, in hospital, the first time in my seventy-four years. I really didn't think there was much wrong with me, although the doctors seemed to think prompt action was required. Either they were being very cautious or something serious was afoot. In no time I found myself on a trolley being pushed into an operating theatre. One of the staff gave me something to drink which he said would calm me down even though I was feeling reasonably relaxed, curious to know what was happening in this, my first visit to an operating theatre.

There was the cardiologist beaming at me and telling he was going to perform an angiogram, a procedure designed to identify any blockages in coronary arteries, or problems with the heart. He inserted a long thin catheter through the artery in the groin and injected a dye to see any blockages on X-rays. I could see the X-ray screen. The cardiologist pointed to a major blockage in the left anterior descending artery, a major artery indeed. He said a by-pass operation was not necessary because the blockage was easy to get to with an angioplasty and a stent. He inserted a small balloon up the artery from the groin. He positioned the balloon across the blockage and inflated it, compressing the fatty deposits and widening the diameter of the artery. All the while, I was being asked if I was experiencing pain. I wasn't.

The drink which was supposed to calm me actually made me chatty and I asked the cardiologist many questions. He was patient at first but then told me to shut up so he could concentrate. That seemed a good idea. A stent had gone up the artery with the balloon. A stent, he explained before he banned questions, is a small latticed tube designed to support the walls of the artery to keep it open and improve the blood flow.

The cardiologist got on with the next patient, and I was wheeled out to the Cardiac Intensive Care Unit where I was monitored for the next twenty-four hours. I was wired up to a drip and a number of monitors checking my blood pressure and heart activity. I was supposed to rest. There was not much else I could do without dragging a lot of tubes and machines after me. People were coming and going. Nurses regularly checked the monitors and the groin area where the catheter was inserted. A Cardiac Patient Educator arrived with a series of booklets giving me guidelines for recovery once I was home. The pharmacist visited twice to discuss the medication which I was to take. A hospital chaplain arrived. Kitchen staff brought meals.

When Jacinta and Angela visited, Angela's reaction was surprise. 'Look at you, Dad,' she said.

There was I, her multi-tubed father in white hospital gown, lying back in bed in a situation she had never seen me in before. She knew a father who had never been ill.

'I can't remember you ever being sick. I expect you to be around healthy and hearty for many years yet!'

'You can see I'm as fragile and as vulnerable as the rest.'

On my first night as a patient, I could appreciate others' comments that sleep does not come easily in a hospital. All through the night a nurse checked the monitors and my groin. Every hour or so, the band around my arm tightened to take my blood pressure. I decided there was not much point fighting the forces of anti-sleep so I did a lot of thinking as I lay there in the half light in my one bed room, the hospital night noises just outside.

Everything had happened so quickly. I needed to take stock. It was hard to think of myself as a heart patient, as having a cardiac disease. I had never been seriously ill. It would appear that the doctors' intervention was very timely indeed. The cardiologist had explained that if a major blockage is left untreated the blood can find other ways through to the heart, just as the water in a blocked river will force its way through running along little creeks. Or the heart may find itself starved of blood and a heart attack even death is the result. In my case the chances of an infarction were high. Like my neighbour Frank, I was a heart attack waiting to happen. In another scenario, my left anterior descending artery could have become completely blocked and, instead of finding another way to my heart, the blood would have been denied access. One massive heart attack followed and in no time I would have joined Maris in the top bunk.

The idea did not disturb me. I was not uncomfortable, anxious or fearful. In fact, my first thought was that I would be joining Maris sooner rather than later and wouldn't have to wait around so long. But now, I was told, the prospects of a full recovery and leading a normal life, given that I take due care, were very good. The indication on the ECG of an earlier heart attack intrigued me. I thought of the broken heart feeling after Maris died. Was that sensation an undiagnosed heart attack? I was under considerable stress at that time. The death of a spouse, particularly by suicide, tops the list of stressors. When I questioned the cardiologist, he said it was a possibility and that the heart may have repaired itself. Can you imagine the girls' reaction when I passed on that piece of news? In a short space of time, they could have not only lost their mother but their father as well. They didn't want to think about it.

I thought of the old bloke dying in front of me in the park at Chambéry. Recently, the husband of a lady I knew suffered a heart attack on the Friday while he was packing the car for the weekend and died the following day. One of my Catenian brothers died on the way to his letter box. I thought of Frank, my neighbour. My life had been under threat. Life is arbitrary. Death comes unexpectedly. Why was I spared and the others were taken? What was I kept alive for? Why was I lucky?

I imagined what sensible Maris would have said if she heard this ruminating. 'Noel, you intellectualise too much. We are all frail humans. Our hold on life is very tenuous. Just be thankful that you're still alive and get on with life.'

So get on with life I did. After twenty-four hours in hospital I was back home, taking it easy for a few days, but soon back to my normal routines, the difference being the medications I was to take for lowering cholesterol and blood pressure and for thinning the blood.

Now when my friends discuss their state of health, I'll have something to contribute. In the meantime, I will welcome each new day as a gift and continue to get on with life.

Epilogue

*Death leaves a heartache no one can heal, Love leaves
a treasure no one can steal.*
— Irish Tombstone

I think of the bushfires that ravage the Australian countryside every summer, leaving a trail of
destruction and desolation in their passage, with
loss of life and property. Little by little, the survivors manage
to overcome their fears and get some order into the devasta-
tion, first of all by removing the debris, then rebuilding what
have been destroyed, replacing lost belongings, replanting
gardens and restoring fences. The scars of the fire storms are
very visible and will remain for a long time in the blackened
forests. But life asserts itself, and the charred tree trunks are
green with new growth.

It is the same with my life.

Maris' suicide was like a fire storm bringing desolation
and destruction. In the aftermath my first thought was how
will I ever survive? Our separation was an enormous hurdle
to surmount. I had to make many adjustments. I could not
grit my teeth and pretend nothing had happened. I had
to overcome a fear of an uncertain future and a sense of

hollowness. I had to ward off despair and face up to my new life squarely.

After the turmoil subsided, calmness was restored and I carried on. Maris' death is a part of my life and I have arrived at a more or less peaceful acceptance. My existence has a new meaning. I have wounds that may never heal, a sense of loss that may never leave me. I can't say that I will ever stop grieving for Maris. I have just got used to the idea of her not being around. Doors have been shut, but, at the same time, others have opened. I have grown. All of this has made me a different person with a different outlook on life and on death. The passion which my sadness has engendered I have directed into my writing and the promotion of my books. I have a purpose in my life, something to look forward to.

I value my spiritual life for the way it has enabled me to erect a barrier of hope against despair. I feel close to reality in my private prayer when I touch the cross that I have worn ever since it was removed from Maris' body, or hold the cross made from driftwood taken from the Oregon beach. It's easy to pray when they are in my hand.

Early in 2008 the incoming Catenian President, Lindsay, rang me.

'Noel, will you take on the role of Secretary for the coming year?'

At first I declined. The job would tie me down and oblige me to attend every meeting as well as having to handle the administrative work in between. But after hanging up the phone, I seemed to hear Maris' voice rebuking me. I rang Lindsay back.

'Yes, Lindsay, I'll take on the job.'

'Thanks, Noel.' I could hear relief in Lindsay's voice. I'm

sure finding a secretary can be hard work. It's a job that most try to avoid. 'What made you change your mind?'

'I appreciate the support the Catenians gave me after Maris died,' I said. 'I regard them as part of my sustaining network. I owe it to the Catenians to give something back in return.'

'We don't keep a ledger, you know, Noel,' Lindsay replied.

'No matter, I'll take it on. Just for one year.'

But this year the incoming President, Tony, in casting around for his committee, asked me to stay on. Tony is a widower of about twelve years. His wife, Eve, is just two rows away from Maris in the Frenchs Forest Bushland Cemetery. Maris and I knew Eve well. They were members of our family group. I witnessed Tony's suffering in the years following her death. I regard Tony as a friend of many years standing. I had the job under my belt, so there I was, the Secretary of the Catenians for another year.

I continue my involvement in Lifeline. I once said to Kathi, the Counselling Manager of our Centre, that a service we didn't provide was support groups for people bereaved by suicide. Later, Kathi approached me. Lifeline Australia, with funding provided by the government, was planning to select certain centres around Australia to run suicide bereavement support groups. Would I like to be involved? I said absolutely. So I underwent facilitation training, along with two of my Lifeline colleagues. Lifeline Australia recognised that among the people who wanted to be involved would be some who had themselves been so bereaved. The groups are open to adults who have experienced the loss of a loved one through suicide. Groups are not for everyone but some people find the experience of someone else who has been through a similar experience invaluable. They can truly understand the shock, the depth of loss and the complexity of emotions felt by family and friends. They find that having a sense of community and support can help to relieve the intense pain associated with suicide bereavement.

I like to think that I contribute on two levels to our groups. In the first instance, I am a trained facilitator and accredited personal counsellor, conscious of the process, sensitive to where the members are at, and keen for them to gain from their presence. But as I am bereaved myself I have a vulnerability to share. I hope to reach out to those in crisis, who may benefit from my skills, experience and wisdom.

I helped design a small brochure to advertise our groups. I am proud of it. We selected a photo of sunflowers for the cover. The sunflower brings an amazing message of hope. In the centre lie up to two thousand seeds, all capable of new life.

*   *   *

Maris' tree is flourishing. My head says I should cut it down before it gets too big. But my heart is listening to another tune. I hear its branches moving in the wind, I love its tall slender beauty. Every time I admire its elegance I see my Maris working in the garden, her pausing to greet me, as I walk from the garage to the house, with her customary greeting, 'How did you go?'

Also by Noel Braun — *Friend and Philospher*

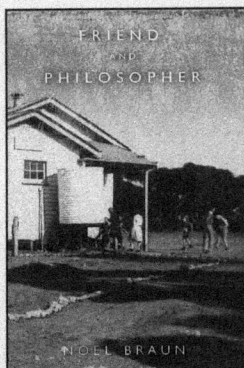

*'The country school teacher should be the
friend and philosopher of the district.'*

Inspired by this message from his college lecturers, the idealistic and zealous 19 year old Doug O'Connor takes up his first appointment to a remote one-teacher school in a decaying Australian country town.

Friend and Philosopher is an honestly written story, told with warmth, tenderness and insight. Entering that painful period when the child must become an adult, Doug encounters a series of reversals for which he is ill equipped, and struggles to come to a better understanding of himself.

Tense and engaging, *Friend and Philosopher* captures the awkwardness and confusion of youth, celebrating the loss of innocence, and dealing with complex and profound issues in a compelling and straightforward way.

"There is a warm irony in the title of Noel Braun's first novel. Braun has not rushed into print. He introduces himself by saying he has been mulling over this book for decades, not years. His story bears the marks of an older man in affectionate conversation with a much younger one. it is impressive.

Set in the early 1950s, this novel is also a paean to a forgotten army of young men and women who, with little more than chalk, went into battle in small country schools. We have plenty of war stories. It makes a change to read about coming of age in the years after World War II.

Doug O'Connor is 19. He leaves Melbourne to take a job in a one-teacher school on the dusty side of Swan Hill, dreaming that his students might come to think of him as a friend and philosopher.

Doug is as green as they come, but there is enough substance in the character for the reader to be prepared to invest in what happens to him."

— **Michael McGirr, *Sydney Morning Herald***

Whistler Street

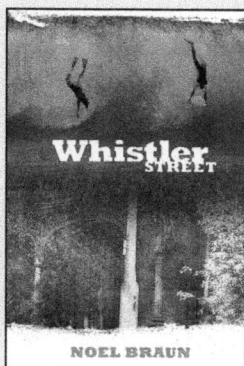

After a childhood in the Western Australian surf, Vince Kelly, burning with a desire to save mankind, enters the Catholic priesthood. In contrast, his beach mate, Jamie Griffiths, lacking any direction, drifts into a disastrous job and marriage.

Following his unwitting involvement in Jamie's mother's death, Vince suffers an emotional and spiritual crisis, shattering all his former rock solid beliefs. In desperation, he quits both Perth and the priesthood. He crosses the desert to Sydney and settles in Manly, hoping to find new meaning and purpose.

As soon as he sees the quaint Federation house in Whistler Street, he knows it's an ideal refuge for his recovery. He transforms the house into a home, makes new friends and begins to rebuild his life but is plagued with indecision and guilt.

Back in Perth the despairing Jamie cries for help. Already guilt-ridden at abandoning his lifelong mate, Vince leaves Manly, painfully aware that on his return he must make some vital decisions about his own direction.

"Braun is a deft writer ... good storytelling ... with a revelation at the end that strengthens the work. A good read."

— **Wendy O'Hanlon,** *Acres Australia*

"This is an interesting story which explores the very best and worst of human nature, warts and all. Emotions such as trust, forgiveness, redemption and despair are fully explored in this new Australian novel."

— **John Morrow's Pick of the Week**

www.ingramcontent.com/pod-product-compliance
Lightning Source LLC
Chambersburg PA
CBHW030918090426
42737CB00007B/231